THE INCREDIBLE SHRINKING MIND

THE INCREDIBLE SHRINKING MIND
What Happens When the Human Equation Gets Lost

Gerald Alper

Routledge
Taylor & Francis Group

LONDON AND NEW YORK

First published 2013 by Karnac Books Ltd.

Published 2018 by Routledge
2 Park Square, Milton Park, Abingdon, Oxon OX14 4RN
711 Third Avenue, New York, NY 10017, USA

Routledge is an imprint of the Taylor & Francis Group, an informa business

British Library Cataloguing in Publication Data

A C.I.P. for this book is available from the British Library

ISBN-13: 9781780491851 (pbk)

Typeset by V Publishing Solutions Pvt Ltd., Chennai, India

For Anita

CONTENTS

Gerald Alper is an internationally recognised psychotherapist, fellow of the American Institute for Psychotherapy and Psychoanalysis, and author of eighteen books, including *The Puppeteers* and *Portrait of an Artist as a Young Patient*. He is a former reviewer for the *Journal of Contemporary Psychology* and is currently based in New York.

PREFACE

As a child, I was fascinated by the idea of infinity. If you came to the end of space and looked out, what would you see? The more I thought about it, the more confused I became.

I was no less confused decades later, when I would encounter the most sophisticated answers on offer to the same, age-old questions. The universe, it was now said, was perhaps a no boundary universe—a space endlessly curving around itself like the surface of a sphere—so that just as it does not make sense to ask what is north of the North Pole, it would not make sense to ask what is north of the universe. Neither would it make sense to ask where space and time come from because, from this unique cosmic point of view, space and time, having no prior existence, would have been created in the thermonuclear moment of the big bang.

Then again, as Alan Guth, the father of the theory of the inflationary universe, has argued, ours could be just one of an infinite series of pocket universes, forever springing into and out of existence. Or, as Leonard Susskind has now proposed, the universe could be a kind of cosmic landscape, a multiverse, and the world we are living in could be just one of an unimaginable, myriad and mind-boggling number of possibilities. Or, last but not least, as Paul Steinhardt and Neil Turok have recently and passionately advocated in their wonderfully innovative theory (and book of the same name), ours could, amazingly enough, be an *Endless Universe*, with not one, but an endless series of big bangs. It would mean something no less revolutionary than that our own Big Bang was not a one-time occurrence. That before our world there was a world out of which our universe emerged. That such worlds are periodically drawn together and collide at regular intervals of about a trillion years.

Profound enigmas such as these could be multiplied a thousandfold in today's world of exponentially exploding knowledge. So it was comforting in a certain way to learn that even at this highest, deepest level there could be nagging and sometimes profound confusion. That Nobel laureate Steven Weinberg, for example, could famously say in *Facing Up* that—when it came to really understanding the fundamental constants of the universe—by the end of the twentieth century a kind of "despair" had settled in among theoretical physicists (Weinberg, 2001, pp. 228–229). And that Richard Feynman, the wizard of a particle physicist and polymathic genius extraordinaire, could seriously wisecrack, "Anyone who tells you they understand quantum mechanics is crazy".

Not surprisingly, scepticism of this order was routinely swept under the carpet by the media. In lieu of daunting puzzles and often disturbing questions, we were fed simple pictures, memorable images, that were closer to cartoons when it came to representing the reality they were supposed to depict. They were neither right nor wrong, just ridiculously incomplete. They were what I like to call *sound bites from the cosmos*, nifty advertising slogans that once heard are hard to forget. In my own field, psychology and psychotherapy, I had personally lived through the arrival of the selfish gene, the birth of sociobiology, the so-called cognitive revolution, the greatly exaggerated death of psychoanalysis, the decade of the brain, the founding of the field of evolutionary psychology, and have presently arrived at the newly christened century of the genome.

During that time, I had conducted literally thousands and thousands of clinical intake interviews of patients seeking psychological treatment. In the course of three decades of private practice in New York City, I had engaged a rich spectrum of mental and emotional duress. I had published numerous books, as well as papers in professional journals, covering many of the major dimensions of psychotherapy with the patients I had treated.

In recent years, however, in order to learn from related disciplines, I had attended dozens and dozens of lectures by world-class neuroscientists reporting on cutting-edge experiments at the interface of clinical psychology and the so-called brain sciences. The meetings, interdisciplinary in nature, were populated equally by scientists and clinicians. Neuropsychologists, cognitivists, experimental psychologists, neurologists, psychiatrists, psychodynamic psychotherapists, and psychoanalysts had joined together in a single hope. To see, if out of an unprecedented open exchange of ideas and methodologies, a common language, with mutually serviceable terms, could emerge. A common language that was not a dumbing down, that did not pander to a single discipline, that, above all, was not overtly reductionistic. Such a common language would be a culmination of a long-sought-after goal, the bridging of the gap between culture and science, something that had never seriously been tried in the life sciences.

Being much more philosophically than technically oriented, my own bias lay with the life sciences. The meaning-making and symbol-forming capacities of the human mind, and especially the dynamic unconscious, were pre-eminent for me. Trained originally as a psychoanalytic psychotherapist, I had lately begun to consider myself as an emerging depth psychologist (which is simply a recent renaming of the more traditional psychodynamic approach). Such an approach is designed to allow the dimension of meaning—nowhere to be found in the brain sciences—to be brought centre stage into therapy. Because people who come to therapy often struggle and are driven to speak from the core issues of their lives, therapists get a precious opportunity to have a ringside seat at what it means to live a life in the real world. For such a therapist, the one-dimensional, toy world rigorously modelled by the experimental psychologist could not appear further from what seems to matter most to just about anyone. By contrast, the less constrained, richer, and broader psychodynamic model is more related to reality, more holistic, narrative, complex, and variable. It is easier to empathise with and to engage for both therapist and patient. It is more receptive to unconscious processes. It intrinsically has more dimensions, with multiple perspectives, built into its basic methodology. It cannot help but be more rooted in intuition and common sense. It is the *natural method* that people—including the most rigorous of scientists—have used when they are trying to convey the sense of something important that has just happened to them. It is, by definition, an interdisciplinary discipline, one that deals with core emotions, core conflicts and core existential issues. That being said, it is worth noting that such a method can incorporate quantitative and experimental methodologies as well—more and more, in fact, it seems to be heading that way—but it is not enslaved by them.

So what was the outcome of this grand utopian project to arrive at an unheard-of common language between science and culture, between the quantitative and the clinical, between impersonal, fact-oriented, third-person objectivity and the meat and drink of life itself—subjective authenticity? I won't say that I was disappointed, because I still faithfully attend such meetings, still expectantly wait to see what lies in the offing, still nurture the hope that, after all, such a project is only in its infancy. But I would be less than honest if I did not admit I had yet to note the barest beginning, yet to hear the faintest whisper of a burgeoning common language. That in place of the promised cross-fertilising dialogue, there was only one-way, didactic lecturing, primarily from neuroscientists to the curious, often raptly attentive, but woefully untutored clinician. That, ironically, instead of a truly invigorating, unprecedented meeting of minds in the life sciences, a dreamt-of electrifying synthesis, there was an undeniably painful clarification, a disheartening but sobering realisation of just how far and how intractably the contemporary balkanisation of the human mind had proceeded.

To show this, there may be no better example than the difference between the way the quantitative, experimental scientist handles emotion and the way the engaged clinician does. For there can be no greater window into the psyche, no greater signature of a person's distinctive subjectivity, than emotion. To the rigorous brain scientist who maps populations of neurons, emotion is a program, involving a computation. An evolutionary animal is, say, threatened by a predator—does it flee, freeze, or fight? There can be no time to think, to weigh possible pros and cons. An unconscious computation must be instantly done, it must make its presence known in the most vivid way imaginable, and, from the standpoint of biological survival, it had better provide the most essentially correct answer for the species in question. For the evolutionary biologist, and evolutionary psychologist, there can only be one answer: instinct in animals and emotions in human beings.

Now what does the psychodynamic clinician, the therapist—who studies people, not neurons, people caught in the unconscious snares of their own tangled life histories—see? Well, they do not see anything that resembles the evolutionary psychologists' account of emotion. They do not see computation. They do not see programs. They do not see elegant mathematical games being ineluctably unfurled. They do see valence or drive—which could indeed be the ancestral manifestation of an original biological imperative to code the particular basic emotion most likely to represent increased survival value. But they see much more. They see something evolutionary psychologists never see. They see nuance. They see multiple, sometimes simultaneous shadings of one emotion blending with another. They do, of course, see game-like behaviour, but they rarely see the kind of precise, machine-like, step-by-step marching to a prescribed goal of which experimental psychologists are so fond.

Although therapists are all too familiar with patients who cannot tear themselves away from their latest, trendiest computer software, who are enslaved by their video games, obsessed with micro-managing every detail of their lives, such addictive behaviour is decidedly not the same thing as healthy social interaction or social relating. And the game-like behaviour they do observe is rarely carried out to completion. Instead, they see games start up, fade away, be interrupted, switch partners. They see the level of concentration and investment of each player in the particular game-like structure dynamically waver and change from one moment to the next. More importantly, rather than economical, mathematical moves—whether consciously or unconsciously computed and then enacted—they see blatantly irrational, self-defeating behaviour. They see firsthand just what happens when supposed experts at game-like strategy—patients who happen to be highly successful lawyers, computer gurus, and financial advisors—try to impose their programmed thinking on the emotional realm in which we all must live. How inordinately inept or even irrational they become when they insist on resolving or clarifying deep-seated emotional problems with the tools of applied logic.

The engaged therapist working in the emotional trenches of real life, in short, can see how easy it is for evolutionary psychologists to make the mistake of assuming they can reduce the multi-faceted complexity of consciousness to the way a computer algorithm solves a problem. And to accordingly treat all mental and emotional dysfunction as though it were at bottom only a troublesome cognitive misfiring, a programming mis-step, a computation gone awry.

I would be encouraged, however, that world-class neuroscientists, at some level, would admit this. I found it endearing that sometimes they would preface their technically awe-inspiring lectures with surprisingly deferent (and human) remarks: "... the reason I took this up, was because I didn't understand people", ... "what you guys do is so much richer than what we do" ... and so on. They recognised, it seemed to me, that to explain how an artificially constructed, toy model of the world with but a single, tightly manipulated variable works is hardly the same thing as peeling away the mysteries of real life.

Science can, of course, not only survive but thrive with the methodologies of computation and quantification, because at some fundamental, informational level, that is how the world works. But as people try to make their way and make sense of the world they find themselves in, they cannot rely on computation. They could not make a single move or action if they did. Nor will it help them to think of themselves as descendants of rodent-like animals, as rarefied federations of genes, products of our neurotransmitters, and functions of our brain modules. They are right to think of themselves instead as profoundly different from laboratory animals. They would not have survived otherwise.

So a question began to form in my mind, which is the basis of this book. Instead of putting the person in the laboratory or in the fMRI machine as the scientist does, why not take the person in the laboratory and in the fMRI machine back into the real world from which he or she came? What would the celebrated scientific experiment then look like if seen—not through the lens of exact quantification and measurement—but through the prism of real life, flesh and blood, psychodynamic therapy? What would we see if, instead of focusing on the precise details of the experiment, we took the fundamental insight into human nature, which it is claiming to have revealed, and reexamine that in the human context of real time and real life.

In short, I want to ask to what extent we need Stanley Milgram and his famous obedience to authority experiments to tell us we are deeply ambivalent when it comes to issues of power and hierarchy? And to what extent do we need Philip Zimbardo and his equally famous Stanford Prison experiment to tell us how susceptible we are to environmental manipulation and insidious brainwashing?

When we look at these legendary experiments by social scientists from the puzzled perspective of real people in real time in the real world, a curious thing seems to happen. Their fundamental insights, appearing neither right nor wrong, begin to pale next to the daunting complexity of the everyday world. By simply holding up the mirror to the contemporary balkanisation of the human mind—from a richer and more meaningful perspective—we see instead a kind of bloodless, X-ray version of the world.

So I am reminded (and reassured) by something R. D. Laing said long ago. You can stare and stare at the slide of a rat brain—*and providing that is all you do*—you will never see a person emerge.

Finally, although hardly pop psychology or self-help, this is meant to be a popular book. To keep it as clear and simple as possible, it is jargon-free. The people portrayed, by and large, are based on actual patients I have known and worked with. They are presented as originally seen by me through the prism of psychodynamic (and psychoanalytic) psychotherapy. Names, of course, have been changed and circumstantial details altered when necessary to ensure confidentiality. The incidents that are described and, especially the psychological dynamics that are depicted, however, are as true as I can make them.

CHAPTER ONE

The psychic rat

This is the creature that has burrowed its way into the minds of patients, that can haunt their dreams, that can induce an almost instant trauma if it turns up unexpectedly in places where it is least wanted. To native New Yorkers, who increasingly find themselves infested with rodents, it may be the most alien life form of all. As a therapist, therefore, over the years I have listened, had to listen, to patients' hair-raising accounts of discovering, disposing of and sometimes finishing off trapped but not yet dead rats.

Here is Marshall on being woken in the dead of night by his wife's screams:

> Maggie had gone into the kitchen because she thought she heard some kind of rustling noise. It seemed to be coming from a sewing basket she keeps on the counter so she lifted the lid. Right there on the bottom was a large, grey rat.

Marshall, a big and burly cabinet maker, pauses and makes a queasy face:

> So I went into the kitchen, and didn't hear anything. I put the lid back on the basket, picked up the basket and carried it out of

1

the house. Two blocks away, I deposited it on the curb and left if there.

He had been content not to know if there had been anything in the basket and more than satisfied there had been no further sightings of the intruder. Several years ago, he had been less lucky:

> I didn't see any, but I knew they were somewhere outside my workshop. I saw the droppings. So, I sprinkled rat poison in some likely places. There was nothing at first … but then … I keep the door open in the summertime … the babies started coming in. They were fat, squeaking and kind of wobbling—I think the poison dehydrates them, drives them out of their nest to look for water before they die. I felt sorry for them. I would scoop them up with a shovel and drown them in a bucket of water.

Less squeamish and more brutally efficient than Marshall was Sidney. Twenty years ago, he and his wife had been fortunate enough to snag a rent stabilised loft in Tribeca and he had no intention of being evicted by a rodent:

> Ann was really terrified of rats and one neighbour after another was telling her stories of sightings. I was worried what she would do if she ever saw one in the loft. When I finally spotted one … just the tail sticking out from behind the kitchen stove … I didn't tell Ann. At night, after she would go to sleep, I would put rat traps out and in the morning, before she got up, I would check them and hide them.
> A week or so later, in the early morning, I was woken by a loud banging. I knew what it was. From the kitchen where I had set the trap was a bloody trail leading all the way to the bathroom. The trap had failed to break its neck, but somehow it had caught it from behind. The front paws were free to try to scratch its way out. I killed it with a hammer, took it downstairs and got rid of it before Ann woke up.

Finally, there was Raphael, who unlike Maggie, Marshall, or Sidney, had never endured an up-close encounter with a rat, but didn't need to. The creature that he said was running around in his head, that kept turning up in his dream, that I call the "psychic rat", had effectively terrorised him. As far as he could remember, ever since he had been a small boy, ever since he had heard that story he could never forget. At sixty, Raphael could easily travel back fifty years in time, to a radio programme called (he thinks) *The Inner Sanctum* and chillingly relive the experience:

I can still hear their voices in my head. Three men, shipwrecked on a tiny island, holed up in an abandoned lighthouse, desperate to be rescued. There is a boat on the horizon, a boat without a living thing on board, surrounded by a black, fan-like wave that is starting to radiate from its hull. The wave, upon inspection, was a swarm, a swarm of perhaps thousands of furiously swimming rats, all heading for the island.

To his horror, it dawns upon the men, that the rats are in search of food on an island that has no food. Panic-stricken, not wanting to think the unthinkable but afraid not to, they begin frantically boarding up every crevice and plugging every imaginable hole in the three-storey lighthouse. Remember the great scene in Hitchcock's *The Birds* where a trapped family try to barricade themselves in their own home against flocks of attacking seagulls gone mad?

Only this is worse. The dread, its presence known, never stops growing. The rats, arriving at last on the island, dash headlong for the lighthouse. What was faint squealing was now loud and cacophonous. Tumbling over one another as they fight to get in, they quickly blanket the outer walls of the lighthouse. At the occasional unplugged crack, red eyes gleam in anticipation. Insidiously, they begin to bore their way through the makeshift barricades.

Listening in a spellbound state, it did not seem possible the men could escape being eaten alive, their bones picked clean. To make the point as gruesomely graphic as possible, a single large ravenous rat finally breaks through. Snatching the first weapon at hand— shovel, crowbar, piece of plywood—the three men, as though defending their lives, hysterical, circle the intruder. A voice like Boris Karloff's sardonically notes: "Three men, banding together, just to kill one rat" ...

And just when the inevitable, hideous outcome seemed imminent, when the vibrating walls seemed ready to burst open ... a strange, flute-like noise is heard ... as suddenly the strident squeaking subsides ... the walls stop quivering ... the rats start leaving. As fast and furiously as they came, they are now swimming back in the direction of the banana boat, laden with fruit, from which the music is emanating.

"Where will they go when they have stripped the banana boat clean?" wonders the narrator in a final macabre musing, "And what kind of cargo will the next boat that arrives be carrying?"

Stories such as these could be multiplied a hundredfold in a city like New York. They illustrate the transformative power of human subjectivity to take a common-place, biological creature, a rodent, and imbue it with an almost mythic symbolism. It is the nature of subjectivity, the first-person perspective, in that everything that happens in our personal world is run through the prism of an utterly unique lived life. It is almost the polar opposite of the third-person perspective, the perspective canonised by science, in which everything in the world is to be seen as only an object, to be studied and observed as dispassionately and impersonally as possible.

A parallel universe

When I consider the relationship of the ordinary person to the wild urban rat and compare it to the relationship of the laboratory researcher and his experimental animal, it can seem I am entering a parallel universe. This lab rat is docile, curious, even friendly. It does not dart. It does not scurry. It does not bite. It does not attack the researcher, who in turn shows no fear, suffers no nightmares, sets no traps, and entertains no murderous thoughts. Not only is the animal fed regularly and generally well cared for (when it is not being surgically operated upon), it is considered a veritable storehouse of indispensable scientific information.

Affective Neuroscience by Jaak Panksepp, one of the world's premier neurobiologists, is considered the bible of its field. It was the first textbook on neurobiology I had ever ventured to read and I was amazed to discover the star of the book was not a person but a rat. Its brain, it seemed, was regarded by neuroscientists everywhere as a kind of Rosetta Stone for ancient, instinctual, mammalian behaviour.

The more I read, the more I was struck by the difference between neurobiology and ethology (the science of studying animals in their natural environment). Ethology, I remembered, had been created in protest and as an alternative to the then fashionable animal experiments of American behaviourists in the early twentieth century. Its founder, Konrad Lorenz, had once famously written that American psychologists "did not know animals". By transporting animals from their natural ecological niches to the artificial world of the laboratory, experimentalists were inadvertently dulling and changing the phylogenetic instincts they were allegedly studying. Indeed, the same behaviour that meant one thing when looked at experimentally in the laboratory could—if allowed to unfold in its natural environment—seem dramatically different. Konrad Lorenz loved to tell the story of what happened when one of Pavlov's experimental dogs—imprisoned in a harness for two months—had one day managed to break free. Immediately attacking what it perceived had been tormenting it, the enraged dog had not only destroyed the experimental setup but invalidated all its supposed results.

The more I listened, the more I wondered why neurobiologists did not pay more attention or at least comparable attention, to the profound differences between animals and people. Why, if the brain of the rat is truly an ancient prototype to our basic instinctual emotional responses—given the unprecedented facility of human beings to anthropomorphise a wide range of both animal and inanimate objects (for example, the sun, moon, stars, wind, seas)—have millions of years of phylogenetic evolution been unable to instill in the human psyche even the faintest empathic resonance between ourselves and the imagined inner world of the wild urban rat?

It was a question I would finally gingerly raise to the great Jaak Panksepp. He had come to New York to lecture on his latest findings in animal research: his controversial discovery that rats reveal the unmistakable beginning of an evolutionary laugh mechanism; that they provide a clear neural prototype for what would become the play instinct in higher mammals, especially humans. To drive home the point, he showed a brief but remarkable film clip: several laboratory rats, experimentally inoculated with the most cutting-edge "play molecules", tumbling and rapturously cavorting around Panksepp's meandering hand, which seemed to lead them like a Pied Piper. Ocular proof, if ever there could be, of how rats really feel about robust play. "They *like* it", Panksepp had triumphantly concluded.

Although as gripped by the demonstration as the rest of the audience, I could not help but wonder: is he saying that he somehow actually *knows*—has an empathic inkling of the inner experiential world of the rat—when it seemingly engages in vigorous playful actions? Is he therefore refuting Thomas Nagel's famous epistemological essay "What Is It Like To Be a Bat?". That even if we could know all the neurophysiology of the bat in the world, we would still be unable to imagine—to somehow identify with and understand what the bat is sensing, perceiving, and experiencing.

But it was the kind of far-ranging, philosophical question that I did not feel ready to raise. If you saw Panksepp, you would know why. Not only is he one of the world's premier brain scientists, but he is a charismatic, Richard Feynman-like scientific presence. Utterly serious, yet fond of joking; supremely self-confident, yet almost avuncular in his desire to share his treasure-trove of knowledge with those less encyclopaedically endowed (everybody else in the world).

So I shelved my question in the Q and A that followed and instead mildly commented that, " ... as a native New Yorker, to whom the wild rat is perhaps the most alien life form imaginable, I could not help but note and be impressed by how extraordinarily loving his personal relations seemed to be (based on the film clip)". Left hanging in the air, waiting to be read between the lines, was the crucial distinction I was beginning to draw in my own mind between the laboratory rat and the "psychic rat" (the rat that is perceived and experienced by you and me, by ordinary people as well as by patients).

After pondering my meaning for a moment, Panksepp thoughtfully said, "Well, I wouldn't want to handle a sewer rat either ... but from a biological standpoint the rat, you know, is a wonderful all-purpose mammal ..." Panksepp, I saw, was trying to teach me, to help me bridge the gap between the world of the neurobiologist and the world of the clinician, to traverse the hundreds or perhaps thousands of evolutionary steps that had to occur over phylogenetic time before these two species could be meaningfully and scientifically linked. His way was simply to assert his authority as an indisputably great expert and international guru in the field, the implication being that it could be done, that it had been done, that he for one had done it. And maybe he had indeed, I thought, maybe he could forge in his mind the hundreds or thousands of necessary links between the rat and ourselves. But, even if so, almost no one else could follow in his footsteps. More to the point, Panksepp had *not* intuited my (admittedly roundabout) meaning. He might be able to bridge species, to actually enter the inner experiential world of the rat, but he had not empathised with mine.

I was left with myself to answer my own question. How do you seriously cross the gap between the subjective and the scientific? Between the indispensable first-person point of view and the equally obligatory, third-person perspective? My book would be my answer, a clinical answer, an attempt to stand up for, to create a space for, the importance of the subjective voice.

For all of their technical brilliance, the neuroscientist, I was beginning to realise, does not really talk about, does not even try to simulate, real life. Although their official aspiration is to interpolate their results into the complexities of everyday life, they are scientifically bound to commence with the simplest, scaled-down models. Time, for example, in the dynamic interpersonal sense is rarely incorporated. The contextual basis of the experiment—the experiential impact upon the subject who is voluntarily participating—is generally disregarded. The psychologists' personality is considered a non-factor, and testers often fail to realise the degree to which the subject may be responding to the experimenter rather than to the experiment. As a rule, the experimental psychologist tends to overrate the neutrality of their stance, and to underestimate how much their so-called objective results are being subjectively tainted.

Unlike the psychotherapist—who is privy to and hungry for every nuance of the patient's thought and feeling—the experimental psychologist is free to be blissfully unaware of what the subject really thinks of the experiment in which he or she is participating. The fact, for example, that patients are accustomed to hearing that psychological tests are frequently duplicitous, contain stooges, are secretive *vis-à-vis* their ulterior motives, are not designed to be empathic, view subjects at best as benign scientific guinea pigs to be handled with care, tend to be disinterested in the fears and anxieties of the participants—other than in specific responses to their own designated questions.

Subjects, in short—and this has been true of almost every patient I have discussed the matter with—sense that whatever they have experienced was much more like *playing a game than engaging in a meaningful way in real life*. It is hardly a coincidence, therefore, that many of the most famous cognitive tests devised not only have a game-like flavour but are literally designed to be taken on a computer. And not surprisingly, participants will sometimes gravitate, get involved, engage, and even obsess on these experimental games for the very same reasons they will take all sorts of analogous games seriously in real life.

Nevertheless, there is a difference, even if the game is tic tac toe, between competing with a person and trying to outfox a computer. Playing with a person means relating to the person as well as to the game. Playing with a computer leaves only you and the computer. From this standpoint, it is easy to see that experimental psychology, perhaps unconsciously modelling itself on our formative years in school, has distanced itself from their subjects' agency and intentionality, treating them instead as third-person objects to be quantitatively measured and explored, but never related to.

Experimental psychology, cognitive neuroscience, social science, and psychodynamic psychotherapy, in their disparate ways, in one form or another, all want to marry the first-person (subjective) point of view with the third-person (scientific) perspective. Although this is a goal I support in principle, it is important to remember that ordinary people on a day-to-day basis do not live, and *do not need to live*, as though there is a clear dichotomy, a rigid split, between the first- and third-person point of view, between the subjective and the objective, and between science and culture. The very fact it takes a deliberate fixing and cognitive focusing of attention to bring such a dichotomy into the forefront of consciousness shows it is neither an unusual nor a natural act.

This is especially clear as soon as one leaves the realm of abstract thought and considers the patient in therapy and simply listens to their voice. For example, the woman who says, "I feel bad today. Why do I feel so bad all the time?" We immediately see, as observers, that she is speaking from somewhere in the context of her lived life, from somewhere in the well of her tangled sorrows, so she is surely speaking from the subjective, first-person point of view. But upon a moment's reflection, we realise, she is simultaneously speaking, thinking about, and describing a particular despairing self, a self that belongs only to her, a self that is herself. So surely she is also speaking from an objective, third-person point of view. Both points of view seem there, both seem blended together, but to a certain degree seem true. A distinction that is inviolable in objective science quickly gives way when looked at from the perspective of everyday life. If this is so, if both are there, does one point of view predominate, perhaps crowd out, the other? Or is it really that there is just one thought, which imperceptibly gives rise to a different thought so that instead of a simultaneity of opposing points of view, we have a deceptive process of very fast-moving but still only sequential thoughts?

It is here that the psychodynamic method that traditionally considers thoughts and feelings from a number of perspectives—from a dynamic unconscious point of view as well as from a conscious one—can help us. Consider, for example, projective identification: a ubiquitous defence mechanism wherein a hated but disowned part of the subjective self—say, a certain bullying, dictatorial, controlling part of the self—is projected upon an other (say, their boss). So that the person is momentarily free to despise, without being aware, what is only a surrogate of an unacceptable, unconscious part of themselves. In projective identification, we see at once how what is profoundly a self–other interaction can be consciously experienced as being about an objective other.

Consider yet another example. A distraught man, who is both angry at his girlfriend and terrified of losing her, says, "All she does is criticise me, 24/7. Is she telling me she wants to leave me?" Although his meaning seems clear, if we ask ourselves—is this man speaking in the subjective or the objective voice—a simple utterance immediately becomes ambiguous. For upon closer examination, there are a number of selves, a number of points of view, cobbled together. There is an angry, complaining self that views itself as being under constant but undeserved critical bombardment. There is a guarded self wary of being blindsided by a traumatic break-up. There is a dependent self fearful of being abandoned. There is a suspicious, perhaps paranoid self straining to read the mind of his girlfriend for hidden clues. And lurking in the background may be a vindictive self already plotting his revenge. This man, then, while visibly upset and speaking in a subjective, complaining voice, is also struggling to gain some objective, strategically necessary insight into the state of mind of his unhappy girlfriend, whom he clearly does not want to leave him. That kind of insight, by definition, is or should be as objective as possible. So the man, in addition to vigorously airing his grievances, wants to be as impartial as he needs to be. And like the first woman, a part of him is therefore trying to rationally study himself, to get a better grip on how this whole mess began.

Just these two examples show how in everyday life—in what William James famously called the "stream of consciousness"—the supposedly intractable points of view of the subjective and the objective, are inextricably linked (James, 1981, p. 219). It follows it is primarily in quantitative and experimental science that they are conceptually sundered and then frozen. It is when the cognitive neuroscientist—stepping back from his own real life in which he like everyone else can effortlessly and seamlessly mix the personal with the impersonal and endeavouring instead to scientifically establish the rigid lawfulness of the subjective and the objective points of view—that the trouble begins.

Having said that, I reiterate that I do not disagree it is a scientifically necessary first methodological step to separate these very different points of view. I only say the time is long overdue to reunite them and that such current interdisciplinary attempts to do so have been essentially in name only.

Here's just one example to show the kind of confusion that can ensue when neuroscientists fail to factor in the human equation. In 1985, in a very famous experiment, Benjamin Libet attempted to investigate nothing less than the neuroscience of free will. Libet took EEG readings of the brain's activities in order to determine the exact moment we become aware of our intention to perform an action, such as raising a finger. Amazingly enough, the results, since corroborated in many labs, showed that approximately half a second passes between our brain's intention to do something and our awareness of doing the same act. It is this delay, according to Libet—the fact we are unaware of the neural activity that precedes our conscious intention to act—that creates the illusion of free will.

This, I admit, is an ingenious and beautiful experiment, especially when studied from the perspective of the neuroscientist. But consider what happens if we look at the very same problem—the age-old question of the existence of free will—from the clinical angle. We immediately see that the patient—caught up in the Sturm and Drang of their private dramas—unlike the professional philosopher or the detached research scientist—seems curiously unperturbed by the metaphysical status of free will. They do not come into the office of therapists in order to discover whether their lives are ruled by free will or determinism. Patients, of course, want freedom, but freedom of a different sort. They want freedom from their inner demons, from their fears, their ego-alien impulses, their obsessive, addictive compulsions, from toxic relationships in which they feel hopelessly embedded, from feelings of inadequacy, of shame that shadow them, from the pressures of who or whatever wishes to control them. But by free, patients mean the ability to act on behalf of their deepest, most empowering interests without the endless worry of unwelcome interference. When that is the case (and it occurs as rarely in therapy as it does in real life) patients—unlike the armchair philosopher or detached research scientist—simply do not care if, at their most unconscious level, it can be shown (by someone such as Benjamin Libet) that they are unknowingly neurally constrained. Do patients, for example, or does anyone for that matter, really care if they are metaphysically free to put their hands into a fire or to jump off a rooftop if they so choose? Have you ever heard anyone complain that they fear they have been programmed by the laws of evolutionary biology to be almost congenitally unable to place their hands willingly into a fire or to jump voluntarily off rooftops (unless, of course, they are under the sway of self-mutilating, grandiose, or suicidal urges)?

Musicophilia

This may be the culmination of Oliver Sacks' lifelong quest, to create what he once called "an existential neurology". I mention it to show that the person-centred, holistic view I am proposing is not a pie-in-the-sky dream to be perhaps realised in the future, but has already occurred a number of times. Not in the life sciences, admittedly, not in neuroscience, psychology, and psychology, but in the outsider world of neurological oddities. It is to Oliver Sacks' lasting credit that he not only transcends but universalises and humanises what for many is a depressing clinical subculture. Reading it, I was reminded of William James's great *The Varieties of Religious Experience*. There was the same wonderful, liquid, and seamless mix of literary grace, narrative flow, telling detail, psychological insight, combined with a unique ability to synthesise a truly encyclopaedic field. And like James, he wears his amazing learning lightly.

The dazzling complexity of Oliver Sacks' mind is manifest in the uncanny way he can come at any puzzling neurological syndrome from seemingly multiple viewpoints. His personal knowledge of the types of musical hallucinations and of the various neurological mechanisms proposed to explain them is bolstered by the over ten thousand letters he receives yearly from every conceivable source (all of whom seem galvanised by the magic and humanity of his prose).

In short, his ability to weave the neural, emotional and subjective components of a patient's psyche into a single narrative tapestry is so outstanding that—after a while—the reader can no longer relocate the familiar borders separating the physical from the mental, and the neural from the subjective. Whereas before Oliver Sacks, it seemed impossible—even for prominent neurologists and psychiatrists to find common ground and a common language—after Sacks, it seemed almost as impossible to imagine the reverse.

That being said, it should be noted that *Musicophilia*, of all Oliver Sacks' books, is perhaps the most formidably technical, the most like a scholarly treatise. In part this may be due to the fact that the author himself is quite musical with a connoisseur's appreciation of the intricacies of the production (as well as the physiology) of musical composition. As a result the book at times can seem self-referential, as though it were intended for a rather rarefied audience: of precociously musical people aware of a subtle or gross neurological musical impairment; and of ever curious neurologists interested in treating or understanding the underpinnings for such a relatively rare malfunction. It therefore lacks the broad appeal of more popular books such as *The Anthropologist From Mars* and *Awakenings*; and is much more in the mode of esoteric books such as his *Island of the Color Blind*; *Diary of a Fern*; and the recent *Uncle Tungsten*.

From the standpoint of our theme, however, what is important is that Sacks—by approaching his patients and their syndromes, howsoever bizarre, from the inside, from the perspective of a lived life—presents case studies that are both deeply personal and highly technical, yet richer and more contextually nuanced than any of his more traditionally fact-based contemporaries. He shows, even in the specialised, often dreary domain of clinical neurology, that it is possible to meaningfully combine the subjective with the objective, to be interdisciplinary in a way that is genuinely humanly inclusive.

The blind Samurai

The psychic rat with which I began was just one of an almost infinite number of objects that get mediated by our psyches. I chose it because it was the best, the most dramatic example I could think of to show the gulf that exists, the split in the contemporary mind, between the subjective and the objective way of perceiving reality. But anything that we know, or think we know, especially something that seems alien, can be viewed in this disjunctive way.

Consider the blind. Notice how wide a berth they are given, how gingerly we treat them, how curiously we look upon them, how silently we pity them. Marvelled at for their faithful seeing-eye dogs, applauded for their will to go on, they are, above all, kept at a very safe distance. Remarkably few people can report a single extended conversation with a blind person; even rarer than that is the person who can claim a blind friend; and has anyone heard of a genuine love affair between two people, only one of whom is sighted (that is, other than in the movies)?

Yet, perhaps most unexpected and startling to encounter is a truly enraged, seemingly out of control, blind person. That at least was the opinion of Sonny, a middle-aged engineering consultant, who had been riding New York City subways for most of his adult life and seen more than his share of intrepid, blind fellow travellers:

The first time I was aware of him I was in the Times Square subway station, waiting for the uptown No. 1 or No. 9 train. It was jam-packed and as the train pulled into the station, and the doors opened, and the crowd pressed forward, I thought I heard a voice from somewhere behind me: GET OUT OF THE WAY ... GET OUT OF THE WAY ... IF YOU DON'T GET OUT OF THE WAY ... YOU'LL GET KNOCKED OVER ...

Well, it couldn't be me he was talking to, I thought ... I make a point of being aware of the space all around me. I try not to push people just ahead of me, even if I am being shoved from behind. I try to get out of the way, if physically possible, of people who are obviously in a big hurry. And I'm never deliberately rude or aggressive if I can help it ... So, it couldn't be me.

But then I felt something stick-like strike my leg, lightly, as a large Jamaican man suddenly charged past me into the subway car. It seemed amazing how fast he was moving, given that the car was packed and that he was obviously blind. The stick that had struck me, or brushed my leg, I now realised had been his cane. As soon as he had occupied the car, he had snapped it shut, in three equal parts, and I remember thinking ... or wondering if he were about to use it as a weapon to assault someone ... But almost as quickly as he had entered the car, he had disappeared ahead, into the interior of the car.

One month later, same train station, same train. This time I was already seated in the rush-hour car. This time I was well out of striking distance when I heard that same lordly commanding voice, from still outside the car. GET OUT OF MY WAY! ... This time I would get a clear view of what had seemed to happen as though in a blur a month ago. The large, light-skinned man who quickly appeared did indeed seem Jamaican or Trinidadian. He had the same three piece cane, already snapped shut and I was taken aback at how confidently he grasped and leaned on the overhead railing. I never cease to be fascinated by blind commuters, audacious enough to ride the New York subways, especially during the rush hours, but there was something creepily different about this man. Everything about him seemed to be saying ... defiantly ... "I am not blind".

It was a signal, unfortunately, the woman sitting directly across from me had failed to pick up. Smiling broadly, as though already anticipating the gratitude she was sure she would receive, she had jumped up and lightly tapped the shoulder of the man, standing to her immediate right ... "There's a seat over here ..."

To the poor woman's total dismay and mine, the blind man was instantly offended: "You're offering me your seat? But why me?"

All the woman could stammer back was, "Well, I thought you might ..."

But the blind man just repeated, "Why me, over all these other people standing?"

I could see the woman was getting scared but she wasn't ready to back down either. "I picked you", she replied as though she were determined to clear up what had to be a misunderstanding ...

That only made the blind man madder, who began leaning his body in the direction of her voice. "But what's special about me?" he persisted. "Why are you ignoring and putting down all those other people?"

By now, it was obvious the woman was being stupid to keep this going, but she answered stubbornly, "I wasn't ignoring anyone ...".

I could not believe what the blind man said next. "I think one of these people should slap your face. You don't act rude, ignoring a whole car full of people. That's not the way I was brought up".

Was he crazy? The thought crossed my mind he might take his cane and swing it like a Samurai sword, a blind Samurai … But the woman continued to act as though she were in an argument with just another difficult subway commuter… . "Now look, mister, …" she said, as though the time had arrived to assert herself. "I don't have to take this from you … You have no more right to speak that way to me than anybody else has!"

"I have every right", he shot back, "to tell off a person as rude and insulting as you… . Do *I* want to sit down? What about the rest of the people?"

I could see Sonny, my patient, a man easily intimidated all his life, months after the incident had occurred, was still mesmerised by the bravado of the man he called "the blind Samurai". Helplessness or gratitude for any service rendered to them, not rage and aggression, was what he expected from an unsighted person. Here, as with the urban rodent, our psychic object overwhelms the objective object. We see what we want to see and have no reason to adjust our impression, unless it is forced upon us by someone such as the blind Samurai. The anger, frustration, and aggression that in various proportions are present in all of us is present in the blind, although perhaps in a more circuitous way. The fact that it is expressed differently and, for obvious reasons, rarely in public does not mean it is not there.

It is only in the psychodynamic framework of therapy that we can elicit and empathically experience the full psychic impact of an encounter with an unaccountably enraged blind person. I did not need to be a rider on the No. 1 train in Times Square or a psychologist concealed behind a one-way glass panel to realise that this blind commuter, who was not only inordinately proud but paranoid, had inexplicably taken offence at the implication he was being offered a seat because he was unable to see. Not recognising the charitable intention underlying the gesture, he had misconstrued it as a demeaning and discriminatory challenge to his rightful dignity. His fanatical determination to maintain his independence takes the form of a pre-emptive strike against what he appears to regard in a paranoid way as an invasion of his private space. In an unconscious act of projective identification, he transfers his own consuming, condescending rage onto the woman who is eager to present herself as a good Samaritan. He then enjoys savagely attacking her. Luring the unsuspecting woman into a heated verbal battle seems to create the reassuring sense of a level playing field, one on which he feels he can win, with his superior rage and aggression. He knows all too well how people are disarmed by a confrontational blind man.

On another level, his outrageous behaviour may mask a need to find his bearings, to make some kind of necessary emotional contact with those whom he cannot see. His aggression may be his way of trying to turn the tables, to force them to declare themselves. He will be the one who occupies their space, who announces himself before they may be aware of his presence. His narcissistic need to command the entire space of the subway car almost upon entering can be seen as a grandiose defence against being shrunken to invisibility—he projects his sense of their invisibility onto them—he imagines they, too, cannot see him. So by turning his handicap into a surprise attack, he startles people by becoming in effect a blind Samurai. He wants his lordly aggression to deflect people away from his lack of sight. He feels empowered only by being abusive. He is infuriated by the stereotypical expectation that he should be grateful for small kindnesses.

There are no doubt other interpretations of this encounter, equally valid or perhaps more so. My point is simply that out of the richly human framework of psychodynamic therapy can come the multidimensional perspective that can do justice and match the complexity of real life. The cognitive and experimental psychologist who tends to rely on the fMRI machine, the rigorously controlled one-dimensional set-up, by contrast, will be in a far better position to interpret the behaviour of simple laboratory animals. But if he or she wishes to extend their results to human beings—and this is the ultimate goal, isn't it?—they must be willing to concede they no longer stand on solid ground. For it is a fallacy to reflexively interpret every psychological finding strictly on the basis of whether or not it tallies with a laboratory animal model.

For suppose the laboratory model and the fully human (psychodynamic) model should clash in their interpretation—and they invariably do—which point of view is to be given primacy? Which will be used to critique the other?

We immediately see the central problem in interdisciplinary thinking: what do we do when the primary assumption of the several models we are fruitfully trying to combine—contradict one another? How do we decide what to preserve in one model, and what to take away from another? How can we determine whether we are being too rigidly reductionistic or too self-destructively revisionist? When we are trying to think in interdisciplinary terms, do we unconsciously or consciously, construct a third point of view, a *meta* point of view—an original cognitive interdisciplinary model—to guide us in designing our new interdisciplinary research?

The psychodynamic method I am proposing has one advantage over the purely neuroscientific approach. It is possible within fifteen minutes of an empathic, sensitive conversation with a prospective patient to learn more about them than a hundred, disembodied fMRI brain slides could tell you. Here we run into the classic problem of the blind physicist who—although he may know everything there is to know about the neurophysiology of the colour red—can never really understand what the colour red means because he cannot experience it. There is an analogy here with fMRI brain imaging, which are basically statistical measurements of regions of neural activity in a particular brain. These slides, which do not reflect *experience*, cannot therefore tell us anything relevant to a clinical, psychodynamic understanding of an individual patient.

The answer, I suggest, is a common language, combining the objective with the subjective, the third-person and the first-person point of view, the quantitative and experimental with the human and psychodynamic. At present, there is no such common language. Instead, there are simple, one-dimensional pictures, culled from cutting-edge neuroscientific research, attractively packaged, and then presented as near-magical windows to the mind. Each of the leading neuroscientists I have diligently followed, listened to, sometimes spoken with, and read in the past seven years, in his or her own way, has seemed bewitched by their chosen window into the mind. Each has tended to regard their own series of experiments to be a kind of narrowing down, a necessary purification of real life—in order to get to an essential underlying principle. Very much like a strobe light (to use the excellent metaphor of MIT behavioural economist Dan Ariely), which slows down light, so as to better study it. But light is one of the fundamental constants, one of the building blocks of the universe. It means, as physicists tell us, that it is incredibly simple. It means what Nobel laureate Steven Weinberg, once said about electrons—(to paraphrase) "Once you've seen one, you've seen them all"—is also true about light.

But the mind we know, far from being simple, may be the most complicated object in the cosmos, with thousands of potential windows into its inner workings. It needs to be understood, can only be understood, if we examine it from the subjective as well as the experimental, quantitative perspective. Which is why I propose we take the person out of the fMRI machine and the laboratory and put them back where they came from, into the flow of their lives.

There will then be at least a chance that—not a better in the sense of a more quantitatively precise—a surprisingly different, more humanly relevant, balanced and less one-dimensional picture may arise.

CHAPTER TWO

If you could save the entire human race from perishing by strangling to death one innocent child …

It was a question no less paradoxical today than when I was a starry-eyed NYU undergraduate majoring in philosophy. The course was ethics, the teacher the late Paul Edwards, and I can still picture the mixture of gravitas and dialectical relish with which he had framed our dilemma. No less earnest than our mentor, we struggled as a class with the impossible question until it dawned on us there was no right answer. It was wrong, of course, to let the human race die; it was more than wrong, it was unthinkable, to strangle to death an innocent child, and perhaps most despicable of all was the one who copped out, who dodged his or her sacred responsibility to make a crucial life-and-death decision by simply refusing to choose.

But to choose, I would passionately argue with myself, was tantamount to playing God, and that had to be immoral. I was not copping out, I was simply listening to the inner voice of my own individual conscience, something that transcended social responsibility. I was making an existential decision that only I could make for myself. I was dealing with a situation that could not possibly occur in real life. After all, there are certain questions, Paul Edwards himself had once told us, that only came up in philosophy classes and this, I decided, was one of them.

19

Years later, now as a graduate student in Long Island University, the same unanswerable question in different guise would resurface. In a class on the psychology of group dynamics, we were unexpectedly presented with a then fashionable game called *Lifeboat*. Five at a time, we were instructed to seat ourselves in any arrangement that suited us, on a plain straw mat, six feet by four feet, placed in the centre of the classroom. We were to imagine the mat to be a lifeboat adrift in the open ocean, ourselves to be the remaining survivors, and the terrible truth to be that there was only room for four of us. Upon the instructor's signal, we had three minutes to either persuade someone to voluntarily leave the boat or to forcefully jettison someone of our choosing. Here, the issue wasn't whether we wanted to do something or not, but to what extent we were prepared to do whatever was necessary to survive. No one, of course, agreed to cooperatively jump off the lifeboat, but what most impressed me was that no one seemed willing to even think about the terrible life-or-death decision confronting us. As though moral reflection, when we were under such dire pressure to save ourselves, was a luxury we could not afford. So there was no pooling of minds, no spontaneous emergence of a heartening democratic process, no debating, no voting. Just an instinctive, herd-like, and panicky rush to do what had to be done, which meant forming an immediate gang of four against a designated and startled victim, someone unlikely in our estimation to offer troublesome resistance. I remember how quickly it was over, how efficiently we had united into a single, lethal battering ram to remove our superfluous passenger—a now helplessly protesting, very scared-looking, not unlikeable, and certainly non-threatening student.

Was it because he seemed the weakest that we had chosen him? We'll never know, because we had been thrown into a situation, euphemistically called a game, that was designed to cut us off from our moral faculty and put us in touch with our supposedly more primitive natures. Then did it mean anything that not one of us had resisted the instructor, had protested that it was the game itself that was immoral, the manipulative attempt to pigeonhole normally thoughtful people into a hypothetical kill or be killed nightmarish scenario where the only choice was which of two homicidal possibilities was preferable? Was the reason I had joined the gang as quickly and impulsively as I did because I had been perversely allowed no time to think, and therefore could not help but be relieved not to have been chosen to be a guinea pig?

I reminded myself I was only a graduate student in a classroom. What I had done, after all, had been just a ploy in a game, not an action with moral consequences in the real world. Given the circumstances, it would have been pointless to risk alienating the teacher by refusing to participate. So far as I was concerned, what Paul Edwards had told us was still true: there are certain questions, and this was another one of them, that only come up in academia.

Over time, the separation between philosophy and real life that I had tried to forge in my mind would be slowly eroded. Game theory, inaugurated by John Von Neuman and Oskar Morgenstern, was becoming a pillar of modern economics, and John Maynard Smith's concept of evolutionary stable strategies (ESS) was beginning to revolutionise contemporary evolutionary biology. Eric Berne, with his hugely popular *Games People Play*, had already introduced game theory into the ego-psychological community.

The appeal of game theory was therefore broad and growing broader. By breaking down behaviour into a few keys and a series of elegant logical moves, it strongly suggests a reduction has been achieved almost as sweeping as that claimed by the animal ethologists with their instinctive behaviour patterns. Yet simultaneously game theory offers the compensating comfort that free will or choice may intervene at any moment in the course of a game: for a player always enjoys the option of being free to elect *not* to play the game. By therefore shrinking the complexity of behaviour to a kind of mathematical, quantitative, logical sequence— while preserving the illusion of existential choice—game theory creates the aura of a virtual psychological laboratory of human behaviour. It gives the sense that all intervening variables except the postulated ones being examined have been effectively removed (and thereby controlled) via the reductionist, mathematical purging of game theory.

Of countless studies, devoted to exploring the intricacies and fleshing out the details of game theory, there is one that especially resonates with our theme. It is an example of a brand new, and fast-growing field variously called experimental ethics or behavioural philosophy. Here it is.

Trolleyology

Imagine this: You are walking along the railroad tracks and you see a trolley car, the conductor slumped over the brakes, heading for an intersection on which five men (oblivious to the danger) are working on the track. On a fork to the left a single man is walking along the track. A switch is in front of you. If you throw the switch the runaway trolley will be diverted from the track on which there are five men to the track on which there is but a single man. One man will be killed, but five will be saved. What do you do?

When put this way, the overwhelming response of the hundreds of thousands of people who have participated in this hypothetical ethical dilemma, said yes. Yes, they would throw the switch. Yes, they would sacrifice one life to save five lives. It was a decision that was arrived at quickly, a decision that struck many as a no brainer.

Now consider part two of the same moral conundrum. This time you are walking along a bridge. Below is the same runaway trolley car, the same brakeman slumped forward, the same five workmen on the track immediately ahead, the same person walking along the track to the left, the same switch, although now far out of reach. But there is a fat man directly in front of you who is sitting on the railing. If you push him off, he will fall upon the track and block the path of the runaway trolley car. Once again one life will be sacrificed, five will be saved.

When put this way, although the moral calculus has not changed one iota—if x is the value of one life, then 5x represents an unquestionably greater value—the majority of respondents say no. No, they will not push the fat man off the bridge. No, they will not sacrifice the life of one to save the lives of five.

Philosophers and cognitive psychologists who have studied this say that it constitutes a bona fide paradox. It is created by two different systems of morality, both of which we carry within ourselves, both of which influence our moral choices. There is an original ancient system which is based on tribal loyalty, on emotion, on kinship recognition. Overlaying that is a modern system of morality, coming at a much later point in our evolutionary development, which supersedes mere tribal loyalties and relies more on advanced cognitive processing than raw emotion.

In the case of the fat man sitting on the bridge, therefore, it is the ancient system which kicks in and says no, I will not kill my kin. I will not kill someone whose face is like mine, whose flesh is like mine, who appears before me, who cannot believe as I cannot that an ordinary stranger will cold-bloodedly take his life. But in the case of the person who is walking along the tracks it is the modern system which is activated and which says yes, I will throw the switch, I will sacrifice one life (someone I have never met, seen, or heard of) to save five lives (five lives, that is, that are totally abstract to me).

Thus do modern philosophers and cognitive psychologists attempt to resolve the so-called paradoxes spawned by studies from the emerging field of trolleyology. Now let us look at the same paradoxes from the much more earthbound, psychodynamic perspective; the perspective, after all, from which the average person intuitively makes his or her way in the everyday world. True to our method, I will take the hypothetical person out of the hypothetical laboratory and put him or her back into the thick of their own real flesh-and-blood lives. I begin by noting I have never met or known anyone who had anything to do with the transit department, with the routing or re-routing of trains, trolley cars, subway trains, track switches, or the like. I have not encountered in thirty years a single patient who found themselves facing anything remotely approaching the kind of Sophie's choice that is routinely thrown at the hypothetical people described walking along the tracks or strolling on the bridge in trolleyology land. No doubt there are people—firemen, policemen, rescue workers, doctors—who on rare occasions are forced to make hard choices about whom to save and whom not to save. But generally, people underestimate just how extraordinary such circumstances are and, as Malcolm Gladwell observes in *Tipping Point*, the great majority of police officers never fire their gun.

So how does the ordinary person, facing the trials and tribulations of everyday life, arrive at a moral decision when facing an ethical crossroads? Perhaps the first thing that strikes the observer is that moral decisions, as a rule, rarely take the form of an either/or, yes/no, binary choice. They are neither black nor white, but grey. When logic is used, it is rarely mathematical—nothing resembling an equation ever comes into play—but tends to be what is called fuzzy logic. Trade-offs are almost always involved, and there is a kind of crude cost-benefit analysis which goes on; but if I had to use one word to characterise the entire process, it would be *ambiguity*.

Now note how different all this is from the moral dilemma as it is framed in the myriad studies coming from trolleyology. You are invited to consider an utterly fantastic situation, that maybe no one has ever experienced, and to pretend that it is happening to you. The effect is to create an immediate distance, a protective shield of unreality between you and the hypothetical experience you are being invited to enter. Implicit is the reassurance that howsoever you respond, you will not be judged or held responsible because there cannot be any consequences to your choices.

Consider how radically different this is from real life where the essence of morality involves accountability for the consequences of your behaviour, which means it is not only likely but inevitable you will be judged. For it is an intrinsic part of forming a moral judgement to have a sense of being on the outside looking in, of appraising someone from the third-person perspective. When that someone is you, we run into the classic psychoanalytic concept of an embattled ego which aspires to the approval of an ego-ideal; a basically amoral primitive id which strives for the pleasures of immediate release and gratification and a punitive conscience (or superego) whose function is to judge. So it is no surprise that guilt or the shadow of guilt is the hallmark of moral decisions.

Note how strangely absent all this is from our hypothetical person walking along the tracks. We are asked in all seriousness to imagine ourselves faced with the mind-boggling dilemma of being in a position to literally save the lives of five innocent workmen or to let them die. To do so, we are asked to consider cold-bloodedly sacrificing the life of one innocent person to save the lives of the greater number. Not only is there no mention of the possibility of a guilty conscience, but it is implied when the question has been answered—not to worry—the conflict, one way or another, somehow will be resolved.

Consider just this one example from real life. A patient comes to the session looking sad and confused. She has just had a terrible accident. Driving home from work, a boy no more than ten has come shooting out on a skateboard from between two parked cars, directly in her path. She slams on the brakes but she cannot stop in time. Her right front fender sends the boy flying backwards, where his head hits and bounces off the cement pavement. She franticly tries to revive him, cannot, and calls 911. The last she sees of him, he is still unconscious and being taken away to the hospital.

As a therapist, I am struck by how tortured this woman is. Although she knows she is a careful driver, who drives slowly and has never had an accident, the thought that accidentally, through no fault of her own, she may have seriously injured an innocent child haunts her. Insidiously, she begins to become paranoid. When the claims adjustor from her insurance company arrives to take her statement, she wonders why his mood seems so strangely sombre. When he tells her, he has no further news as to the condition of the boy she hit, she senses he is hiding something. When in the months to come, she continues to hear absolutely nothing concerning the condition of the boy or even the status of her accident, she begins to suspect a conspiracy of silence. More and more, a gruesome thought begins to pop into her mind: "Is the boy dead?"

If she wanted to know, she could find out, but she really does not want to know. It is unthinkable to her she may have actually killed a child, which she has to realise on some level is a distinct possibility. But she does not want to face her guilt, which she fears would devour her. She is never investigated or charged for negligent driving, but she cannot escape the eerie thought that her car may have been the agent of a boy's death.

Or consider a very different reaction, a reaction of morbid excitement to a freakish occurrence. Ralph, a hyper young salesman, has been taking a lunch break with his friend, Pat, who is also the manager of the company they both work for. They are sitting on a bench, near a waterway, under a small bridge, when they hear, then see, a tremendous splash. Incredibly, a car has careened over the side of the bridge, head-first into the water not twenty-five feet away. Were the driver and any passengers in the car lucky enough to be thrown clear on the bridge or are they now trapped in the slowly disappearing car? They cannot tell. Ralph, who feels disoriented by the unreality of the scene, looks for guidance from Pat, a former Green Beret in Vietnam, who is fond of recounting tales of jungle derring-do. But Pat, saying and doing nothing, shrugs off his responsibility. It appears neither of them feel obliged to act or get involved in any way. Who could possibly expect them to dive in the water and risk drowning in a futile attempt to pull people from a possibly empty car? They are like roadside spectators who suddenly find themselves eyewitnesses to a tragic car accident. For fifteen minutes until their lunch break is over, they watch in quiet fascination as a crowd gathers, a police car arrives, and a fire truck drives up. Then, with the car fully underwater and no survivors in sight, they go back to work.

Trains are not cars, and the psychology of trains is different from the psychology of cars. It is true that daily commuters in New York City are wary of underground subway trains. Horror stories of people being pushed from the platform by psychopaths before incoming trains have been imprinted in their psyches. If you ride subways as I do, look closely and you will see how carefully people backpedal from the edge of the platform as the train begins to pull in. If you ride enough trains, it is only a matter of time before you see the sickening sight of someone, their hand or arm trapped in the closing doors, in danger of being dragged by a train that is about to pull away. You see defiant teenagers, recklessly riding on the outside in the dangerously narrow space between two cars. You hear the voices of infuriated passengers, crushed together in the rush-hour traffic, who have been pushed one time too many, threatening to "bash someone's face in". You hear droning public announcements reminding us to "watch your belongings" and, increasingly since September 11, "if you see something, say something". You see the large posters warning us that any suspicious-looking package we may be carrying is subject to police search at any time. And you realise, if you are not wary to begin with, it will not be long before you are made so.

How different all this is from the conventional trains that carry people or freight that ride above the earth on rails in the open air. Here we encounter the iconic images of myth and fiction. The train that roars and whistles in the lonely night, that thunders out of the Old West, that flashes along gleaming steel tracks that never seem to end. This is the train that people do not worry about. They do not see themselves falling under its wheels. Although fear of flying is a widespread phobia— in spite of the well-known fact that the odds of dying in an aeroplane crash are less than one in a million—they do not seem to see themselves perishing in a train wreck.

With that in mind, try to imagine now a real person, yourself or someone else, walking along the tracks and encountering an actual runaway trolley car, with the conductor mysteriously slumped over the brakes. A trolley car, of course, is not a subway train, a commuter train, or a freight train, but a single car, presumably chosen to lend plausibility to the hypothetical and far-fetched idea that a passerby could conceivably have a chance of resourcefully diverting its path. So let us say, you are walking along, you see the runaway trolley car, you see the five workmen in imminent danger, you see the nearby switch, and your instinctive response is to throw the switch. Now imagine really throwing the switch. Do you happen to know how to do that? Have you ever done it before? Do you turn it to the right or the left? Do you push a button or do you do it manually? Is it indicated clearly what exactly is required in order to divert the trolley car from the track it is on to a side track? Are there written instructions or unambiguous signs to direct you? Is there realistically time enough to decipher how to throw the switch, to throw it and to save the five workmen? How do you know that the workmen at the very last moment will not jump from the tracks rendering your actions unnecessary? So that not only will you have accomplished nothing but if you have succeeded in diverting the trolley car you will have pointlessly killed the innocent man who happens to be walking on the side track.

Or consider the fat man sitting on the railing on the bridge. Much as the idea repels you, you are prepared to push him off the bridge if that is what it takes to save the five innocent workmen. But how do you do that? Do you sidle up to him, trick him, or charge at him? Do you know how much force it takes to push him completely off the bridge? Have you already calculated if the time it takes the fat man to fall on the tracks will be less than the time it will take the runaway trolley car to reach that same point on the tracks? Do you really understand the physics involved? What if the fat man, seeing your intention, resists or tries to drag you with him? What if you do push him off, not onto the tracks but on the ground nearby, so that once again not only have you accomplished nothing but you have managed to murder an innocent bystander?

Note that so far we have talked only about the mechanical and logistical difficulties confronting someone who has decided to rescue five endangered workmen from a runaway trolley. Note that the dynamic element of time so far as the thoughts and feelings of the person who is making the decision has been given short shrift. As though the rendering of a moral judgement, one that carries the gravest consequences, is not a process which is intrinsically fraught. As though the fact there is only an instant to decide somehow exempts the person—regardless of their choice—from an aftermath of retrospective rumination filled with recrimination, rationalisation, anxiety, and guilt over possible wrongdoing, not to speak of the fear of social and legal reprisals.

The moral dilemma posed by the hypothetical example of the runaway trolley car glosses over the fact that in real life it is extraordinarily difficult to induce an ordinary person to render a life or death decision concerning another human being. Think of the threat of imprisonment that has to be dangled before able-bodied citizens to induce them to serve as jurors in criminal cases. Think of what the army recruit must endure in boot camp in order to acquire—whenever necessary—the proper killer instinct. Then think again of what this hypothetical person is really being asked to consider: to make the most horrendously difficult decision, in less than a second, they will perhaps ever have made in their life.

Seen this way, the person who is being asked to choose in this way is being treated as a kind of one-dimensional creature. As if they have just been given an elementary problem in mathematics or logic. In order to make the inquiry scientifically respectable, the attempt is made to operationalise the steps of the decision. Accordingly, they do not ask how someone feels, just what judgement would they render? As though moral judgement and feeling could not be—as is so often seen clinically—seriously at odds.

Needless to say, the psychodynamic view reveals a very different process, with moral judgements and feelings freely intermingling, entailing multiple points of view, all dynamically shifting and interacting—with now one, now the other in the ascendancy. While trolleyology, by contrast, tries to freeze a potentially potent psychodynamic process into a single, unchanging moment in which everything is put on the *correctness* and subsequent justification of the response (because so many consequences would flow from it). In other words, from the mindset of trolleyology, arriving at a moral decision is not unlike an inner trial in which one's behaviour, or single choice, is supposedly rigorously examined, according to some internalised approved-of standard, and then duly judged. Here trolleyology, like our own lofty theory of jurisprudence, tends to divorce the behaviour that is being evaluated from the context in which it arose. Like a miniature court of law, it tends to deny that everyday morality in the real world, more often than not, is *situational*.

Moral Minds

From so simple a beginning as a wandering passerby and a runaway trolley car, serious philosophers and cognitive scientists have drawn sweeping conclusions. Mark Hauser is an evolutionary biologist who is a consummate scholar of the mind sciences. His magisterial book, *Moral Minds*, is an encyclopaedic survey of ongoing, cutting-edge, interdisciplinary researches into the origins of moral behaviour. This includes his own exhaustive administration of the now classic trolleyology questionnaire—via the internet—to an international audience comprising, literally, hundreds of thousands of willing correspondents. He believes the kind of standardised computerised data thereby made available provide, for the first time, the basis for a scientific study of the process of making moral judgements. Scientific and objective, according to Mark Hauser, *because* it is impersonal.

Yet, from a psychodynamic point of view, this can hardly be the whole story. To ask someone to choose whether to save one life or five lives is to ask someone to project themselves into the most highly charged and conflictual situation imaginable. A situation that cannot fail to elicit personal emotion, as well as the (dearly sought-after) so-called moral reasoning. The fact that both question and answer are subsequently tabulated and then standardised does not so much place it in the realm of scientific studies as to trivialise it. Note, for example, the rapidity, already mentioned, with which the majority of subjects replied. Does that reflect the sure-footed, instinctive response that the same person would presumably make if they were in the actual situation described? Obviously not.

We begin to see why the trolleyology questionnaire is so handily computerised and why it can seem to resemble a video game more than a situation with which one can identify in real life. By positing a separate moral faculty, in the same sense that famed linguist Noam Chomsky posited a separate language faculty, Mark Hauser hopes to segregate our deepest emotions from our weightiest moral judgements. He overlooks how much more revelatory and universally applicable can the moral odyssey of just one person be—a Raskalnikov, for example, in Dostoevsky's great *Crime and Punishment*—especially when set against the soulless computerised inventory of disengaged random respondents. Compare, for example, responding to the trolleyology questionnaire to spending just one afternoon in Walter Reed Hospital for wounded veterans. Or imagine actually pulling the switch and having to watch an unsuspecting lone victim being swept under the wheels of the now successfully diverted runaway trolley car and gruesomely dragged to his death. Is that an experience one can ever forget?

What the psychodynamic method immediately makes clear is the difference between being *immersed* in an authentic real life moral crisis, from which all kinds of repercussions must follow, and being safely disengaged: such as participating in the trolleyology study. The moral faculty in certain fundamental ways does not operate like the language faculty. A wrong moral judgement can produce a lasting insidious effect, while no one can be traumatised by a grammatical mistake.

It follows that moral judgements are innately charged, filled with emotion. Unlike language use which serves more cognitive and instrumental ends, moral judgements tend to involve life or death (fight/flight) issues. To the extent they are about biological survival needs, they are more primitive and in that sense moral judgements may be closer to the religious impulse than to disembodied language use. Which may explain why our so-called ancient morality—our ancestral tribal loyalty to those we recognise as our kin, such as the fat man sitting on the bridge—can, in certain circumstances, strike us as the very heart and soul of our morality.

To show how divorcing the moral faculty from the emotions—far from leading to clarification of the underlying principles—can instead create unnecessary confusion, I would like to mention just one further example. It is borrowed from *Moral Minds*. A mother tells her small son, Fred, to share his bag of candy with his friend, Billy. When Fred gives a single piece and Billy says, "That's not fair", the mother agrees. Fred is then likely to conclude that, "When it comes to sharing, everyone gets a fair share" (Hauser, 2006, p. 163). The only way Fred could reach such a generalisation, according to Mark Hauser, would be if such knowledge were innate, because it was not present or available from the environment—certainly not in Billy's single statement, "That's not fair". It is the characteristic of an innate faculty, he notes, for there to be *more output than input*.

Mark Hauser is assuming that categorical knowledge—such as the generalisation that it is *always* unfair not to share with your friends—can only come from (a) learning a categorical statement or (b) from innate knowledge. By learning a categorical statement, Mark Hauser seems to mean something like Fred having heard his mother on certain occasions explicitly say, "It is always unfair not to share with friends like Billy". He does not consider that there are many ways, other than the articulation of explicit categorical statements, for Fred to learn the indispensable social principle of reciprocity.

Fred may, for example, note that his mother always makes a point to share generously with those around her. He may have noticed that, whenever his sister shares with her friends, his mother beams approvingly. He may be aware of other friends, besides Billy, who plainly get angry when their friends won't share. He may have observed, on certain occasions, the attribution of the word 'selfish' to those who hoarded their food. He may recall, suddenly, that every time he himself did share, he was in some way rewarded.

In short, there may be numerous plausible experiential and behavioural ways from which Fred could infer the alleged categorical knowledge. Mark Hauser overlooks just how important learning the principle of reciprocal altruism is to our social education and concentrates instead on the supposedly universal moral principles that so intrigue moral philosophers. He thereby disregards the possibility of a psychodynamic contribution: the wealth of unconscious communication and emotional signalling that is always going on. He seems to rely, so far as the moral faculty is concerned, on one-dimensional, linguistically cognitive informational exchanges.

Evolutionary psychology

As mentioned, there is currently an unprecedented joining of hands by evolutionists of all stripes and moral philosophers. There is, for example, Johnathan Haidt, a moral psychologist. In his recent book, *The Happiness Hypothesis*, he constructs a broad evolutionary view of morality that traces its connections both to religion and politics. He posits two separate mental systems, already alluded to, that drive morality: an ancient system and a modern system. The ancient system relies on moral intuition. It is characterised by emotionally laden behaviour, primitive gut reactions, and occurs almost instantaneously. The modern system, comprising what we call moral judgement and what Mark Hauser calls the moral faculty, came after language: when "people became able to articulate why something was right or wrong". What Johnathan Haidt memorably calls "moral dumbfounding" arises when moral judgement "cannot come up with a convincing explanation for what moral intuition decided" (Haidt, 2011, p. 27).

From this point of view, there could not be a better example of "moral dumbfounding" than the paradoxical responses to the trolley-ology questionnaire. It is our modern system of morality, on the one hand, that tells us it is acceptable to divert the train switch—to kill one person in order to save five. It is our ancient moral system, on the other hand, that tells us it is unacceptable to physically throw one innocent person onto the track in order to save five. And it is because we cannot articulate the roots of our manifestly contradictory behaviour that we experience moral dumbfounding.

According to Johnathan Haidt, it is the ancient moral system, lagging behind the modern moral system, that is causing the problem. Evolutionary studies of the origins of morality have led him to conclude that this ancient system is itself comprised of five separate instinctive systems that are innate: (1) "Purity and Sanctity": a taboo against any excess that might contaminate the group and a drive to bind people together through common rituals; (2) "Loyalty to the In Group": an instinct to be vigilant in punishing slackers, freeloaders, traitors and anyone whose actions undermine the group's cohesiveness; (3) "Respect for Authority": an instinct to defer to those above you in social rank and to offer protection to those below you; (4) "Do No Physical Harm": an instinct to protect others, especially your own kin and those who are vulnerable; (5) "Do As You Would Have Done To You": no less than an instinct to obey The Golden Rule (renamed by evolutionary biologists as reciprocal altruism).

By way of contrast, the famous primatologist, Frans B. M. de Waal, does not believe that the evolutionary purpose of morality is to suppress individual selfishness. Many animals, he feels, show empathy and altruistic tendencies but do not have moral systems: "For me, the moral system is one that resolves the tension between individualised group interests in a way that seems best for most members of the group, hence promotes give and take".

Yet another voice is science writer Jim Holt. In his *New York Times Magazine* article, "Good Instinct: Why Is Anyone an Altruist?", he questions the prevailing assumption that altruism is best understood as an urge wired into us by selfish genes. He points out there may be instead, as the philosopher Thomas Nagel has noted, a rational, objective reason for altruism, one rooted in "the conception of one's self as a person among others equally real".

Here, the implication seems to be that we don't need selfish genes to wire altruism into our brains. The philosophical, rational side of our minds, in our calmer, more mature moments, can do the job. As though we are a race of philosophers—sufficiently detached from our biological drives—who are perfectly capable of acting upon a morality dictated by disembodied logic. Forgotten are the inconvenient facts that: while a minority of people can say no to the urgings, for example, of their reproductive genes (and practise strict birth control), the majority of people cannot (otherwise, there would be no overpopulation); and that it is simply naive to think that a so-called "objective altruism" unfettered by biological constraints could compete, on a statistical basis, with hardwired genetic altruism with its immediate, self-reinforcing "warm neural glow (as measured by brain scan experiments)".

Finally, last but not least in our necessarily brief survey, there is Harvard psychologist, Daniel Gilbert, who has posited what he calls "a happiness set point"—the baseline position to which we keep returning, regardless of whether the news is good or bad, in a surprisingly short time. In part, this is because, as Gilbert notes, we are not very good at what he calls *affective forecasting*—the ability to predict what makes us happy or unhappy. In addition we suffer from *durability bias*: the tendency to overrate the staying power of any particularly strong emotional state of mind we happen to be in. In turn, this promotes what he further calls *immune neglect*: where we insufficiently appreciate the ability of our considerable psychological immune systems to protect us against all kinds of narcissistic injuries.

Daniel Gilbert, in other words, is pointing out how inadequate we are when it comes to predicting our affective future. Which is to say we can't really know how we are going to experience something, particularly something of emotional significance, until it happens. Which of course only means that we can't prognosticate the future. Or, to put it in psychodynamic terms, our private fantasy of some important, impending event will almost always be dramatically different from our actual experience of it. But is there anything we're good at predicting? To say we're poor at affective forecasting is to imply we're good at some other kind of forecasting. From a psychodynamic point of view, what is therefore interesting, is that even though people do not know what they really want or don't want, their appetite for fantasising about their future remains undaunted.

After reviewing all of this, and much, much more, Mark Hauser concludes his encyclopaedic *Moral Minds* this way: "The systems that generate intuitive moral judgements are often in conflict with the systems that generate principled reasons for our actions, because the landscape of today only dimly resembles our original state" (Hauser, 2006, p. 418).

Mark Hauser seems to be saying that our principled modern morality represents a moral advance over our ancient tribalism. He seems to overlook the psychodynamic truth that in real life the overwhelming majority of people are rarely forced to play God with the lives of others. That the instinctive, intuitive feeling of most people that there is almost nothing that could justify strangling an innocent child to death—in spite of the fact there may be extraordinary circumstances in which our social conscience demands such a sacrifice—actually represents the soul of morality (its driving force). That as opposed to the wire-drawn scenarios of trolleyology, moral choices are seldom binary and almost always complex. That the essence of morality, especially from a psychodynamic perspective, is therefore emotion, tribalism, ambivalence, contextualism and, above all, social embeddedness. That once you remove the social context—face-to-face recognition, identification of kin—you are also removing an indispensable part of our morality, which derives from our ancient system. That no one really ever made a moral decision based on a decontextualised calculus of xs and ys, of pluses and minuses, of supposedly quantised moral units. That to thereby try to decontextualise and deconstruct a flesh-and-blood moral choice is to render it into an inanimate computer game, a kind of virtual reality. That the ancient and modern systems of morality do not just conflict with one another (as they undeniably sometimes do) but generally work in concert or at least try to. Which is why, in the realm of moral decision-making, ambiguity is the rule.

So, what have I learned in the decades since I took Paul Edwards' undergraduate philosophy course? Well, I can still think of no circumstances under which I would strangle to death an innocent child. I doubt I would pull the switch either to sacrifice one innocent person to save five. If I were forced by extraordinary circumstances to play God, I would probably freeze, as I think most decent, sensitive people would.

If I learned anything, it is probably that *you cannot quantify moral truth*. It is, of course, wrong to sacrifice an entire group of people to save one or several individuals who happen to be most precious to you. That way lies the madness of tribal fundamentalism. But it may be equally wrong to sacrifice a substantial number of people in order to save an even greater group. That way lies the madness of a runaway nuclear arms race.

The answer, at least, is complex and lies somewhere between the ancient system and the modern system of morality. Between the tribal fundamentalism of our most primitive constructs and the disembodied compartmentalisation of our high-tech, computer-driven modern world. But if you doubt that and think—at least in the exceptional case of the hypothetical person strolling along the tracks who spies a runaway trolley car—it is as clear-cut as trolleyology would have it, ask yourself this:

Is there any difference between the logic telling you it is okay to sacrifice one man to save five (one x to save 5x), and the logic in 1945 telling America it was morally just to save three million American lives (the estimated cost if we were forced to invade Japan) if all we had to do was to drop one atomic bomb on 250,000 innocent people in Hiroshima?

Obedience to authority

In the 1960s, Stanley Milgram, a Yale University social psychologist, decided to test the limits to which ordinary people could be made to conform to authority. Milgram's subjects were local townspeople from nearby New Haven and Bridgeport, who had responded to an advertisement in a local paper asking for volunteers who would participate in "a study in memory". Subjects were to play the role of "teacher", while someone else (secretly Milgram's confederate) was to play the learner. Supposedly, the learner was to memorise a list of word-pairs and it was the job of the teacher—seated out of sight in another room—to help him by delivering an electric shock whenever an error was made. The more errors that were made, the stronger the shock that was delivered. All the shocks were delivered by the volunteer experimental subjects who were seated before a box with switches labelled *Slight Shock, Moderate Shock, Strong Shock, Very Strong Shock, Extreme Intensity Shock, DANGER: Severe Shock XXXX (450 volts)*.

No shocks, of course, were actually given. The response that seemed to be coming from the learners were from a tape recording with prearranged right and wrong answers. As the errors mounted, so did the punishment. Subjects would hear unnerving screams of pain, demands to be let out, and, eventually, in the worst-case scenario, silence. When subjects hesitated and protested against delivering the next level of shock, they would be strongly exhorted by the experimenter to continue: "Come on, come on! You must continue! It's all right!" This, of course, was the true purpose of the experiment: to see how far the subject would go in giving someone (potentially lethal) electric shocks, when prompted to do so by an authority (the experimenter).

When asked to guess the number of subjects who were willing to continue right up until the lethal 450 volts, the usual estimate is only 1 per cent. In fact, about 65 per cent did so.

This result would astonish Stanley Milgram, the community of mental health professionals, trickle into the national consciousness, and over time became one of the most famous experiments of the twentieth century. Tirelessly referred to, it has been cited as evidence to support: the alleged potential for totalitarian abuse available to anyone in a position of authority; the amazing susceptibility to manifestly barbaric brainwashing of the ordinary person; the capacity for sadistic, evil acts of the ordinary person, given the right situation; and so on.

Readers who have stayed with me so far will not be surprised I think there may be perhaps another way to look at Milgram's results. That way, analogous to our approach to trolleyology studies, is to look at what Stanley Milgram claims to have done—not as a devilishly clever, devious experiment by a brilliant social psychologist (which he undoubtedly is)—but as a legitimate slice of life, supposedly occurring in the context of the real world, which is how it presents itself to its unsuspecting subjects. And from that perspective, the first thing that strikes the informed observer is just how phony this experiment really is. From the ad appearing in the local newspaper, to the role played by the experimenter, the role played by the subject, the role played by the learner, the role played by the machine supposedly delivering electric shocks—nothing is what it seems to be. The ad is a decoy, the experimenter does nothing but lie to the subject, the subject is instructed at the outset to be an imposter, the learner is an actor, the screams and protests that are heard are pre-recorded and, most crucially, not a single electric shock is ever delivered. So I will ask the obvious question. Given the hokiness of the set-up, are we asked to believe that the experimenter and stooge-learner were such masterful actors that not one drop of suspicion crept into the minds of the understandably dumbfounded participants? Isn't it just possible that on some deep level—which is what I believe—that the participants sensed that whatever was happening, it somehow wasn't really real? That the learners who were faking screams of anguish, protests of torture, and in some cases incipient heart attack, weren't in all that much trouble? That no one was actually going to be electrocuted? That this was a learning experiment, wasn't it, and who ever heard of anyone dying in a learning experiment? That when the experimenter repeatedly reassured the panicky subjects that "everything was all right", he knew what he was talking about, he was the expert, wasn't he? In exactly the same way that a person, certain he or she is exhibiting all the symptoms of a potentially fatal heart attack, is immediately reassured by the examining physician, who calmly reports, "No, you're just suffering from heartburn"? That whatever was going on, there would be no consequences: no police investigation of possible criminal negligence; no aftermath of any kind; that the only thing that would happen when the experiment was over would be that the subject would go home?

So I do not think Stanley Milgram's electric shock experiments, ingenious though they are, reveal some latent streak of sadistic depravity in the heart of humanity waiting to be tapped. What they do show is what happens when all the dependable social cues on which people normally rely are suddenly yanked away—you find yourself confronted with a life-threatening situation—and you have but a moment to react. Think of someone shouting "FIRE" in a crowded cinema, someone shoving a gun in your belly and asking for your money, or seeing a runaway trolley car on the brink of slaughtering five innocent workmen. I've never had to face any of those situations, never heard of anyone having to, and the chances are neither have you. Certainly, none of the participants who responded to Stanley Milgram's ad had ever before encountered a psychological experiment remotely like this one. And since a part of the protocol was to deliberately rush the participants as much as possible, they literally had but seconds to make up their minds. Put yourself in their shoes. Having no frame of reference whatsoever with which to appraise the situation, the only thing they could trust was the presumed expertise of the experimenters. If he didn't know what to do then no one did.

From the psychodynamic perspective, Stanley Milgram's experiments show—if you are willing to take whatever Machiavellian steps are necessary—how to get someone to do something they really don't want to do. You rush them to the point of panic, you bully them, manipulate them, you do whatever you can to elicit the herd-like, follow-the-leader response. So, yes, Stanley Milgram's experiments, and countless others that followed in his footsteps, reveal an embarrassing human propensity for mindless conformity. But didn't we know that already? Note, also, not only how dark, but how limited is Stanley Milgram's view of our susceptibility to obedience to authority. He does not consider the lifelong socialisation process—to which every human being is subjected from the moment of birth—the ways in which society trains and indoctrinates its constituents in the protocols of proper obedience to the perceived constitutional powers that be. He does not consider what every psychotherapist is privileged to see: the lifelong struggle to rebel against the very same urge to be obedient. How the infant, soon after its honeymoon period of surrender to its omnipotent parents, begins its universal quest for separation and individuation. How childhood, adolescence, adulthood, middle and old age, to a great extent, are a never-ending and defining balancing act between identification and individuation, between the need to merge, sometimes to surrender to the prevailing group, and the need to stand alone.

Finally, in terms of our theme, we can see how evolutionary psychologists, neuroscientists, and social scientists, in their efforts to understand the origins of good and evil, of moral and immoral behaviour, have tried to quantify moral truths. The pictures they present, so-called windows to the human mind, intelligent and ingenious though they may be, pale in complexity next to the details, the variances, and the nuances of real life. But it is the nuances of real life—not the mechanical understanding of what at this pristine stage is only a toy world, a one-dimensional, artificial, laboratory experiment—that we are trying to fathom. For that to happen, we need in addition to the wonderful mind-probes of high-tech, contemporary neuroscience, the psychodynamic understanding that can only be grounded in the indispensable context of the real world.

CHAPTER THREE

Homo economicus

Trust, above all things, was what Charlotte valued. It was what had kept her for over twenty years at the small Manhattan publishing firm that had hired her soon after she had graduated from City College. She trusted, in spite of the dismal rate of pay, that they truly believed she had the makings of a first-rate fiction editor. It was trust that was the indispensable glue for any durable, authentic relationship, and it was exactly the missing ingredient that explained the ultimate failure of her first marriage. It was what had emboldened her, only a week after she had opened up her first savings account, and against all her normal cautionary instincts, to invest in Pax World. After all, she had proudly told me, thirty-seven years ago this had been the first company to introduce socially responsible mutual friends in the United States. And for nearly twenty years, Pax World had repaid her trust, slowly but inexorably, seemingly managing itself, more reliable and trustworthy than any single person she had ever known.

So she could not have been more dumbfounded and felt more blind-sided, shortly after 15 September 2008, when—goaded by the financial panic that was tearing through the country and nervously realising she simply did not know the current value of her investment—she decided to check her portfolio.

As Charlotte would tell me:

> In one fell swoop I had lost twenty thousand dollars of what essentially is my life's savings! I couldn't believe it. Don't panic, think long term not short term, eventually the market goes up. That's what I believed, that's what they always told me, that was my mantra. 'If you sell now,' the woman at my bank whom I trust, gently warned me, 'You'll lose a lot of money. Sit tight, let's see what happens.'
>
> But sitting tight meant losing over a thousand dollars a day and, try as I might, I just couldn't do it. After only five days of seeing the investment that had been my rock for twenty years continue to sink like a stone, I hit the panic button. Amazingly, with just one phone call, one electronic transfer, I was able to place all of my remaining savings into a permanently FDIC insured, money market account. I can breathe again ... but lately I am beginning to second guess myself. What do *you* think? Will I realise one day that I made a terrible mistake?

I know nothing about financial investments, have never been a player on the stock market, but I did not hesitate to tell Charlotte that, in her case, I felt she had made a sound decision. Her case, of course, is that of someone who, though not impulsive, is prone to anxiety, has trouble waiting, expects little from life, and gets easily discouraged. The lynchpin of her momentous financial decision was her astute realisation that no amount of money could be worth the agony she undoubtedly would suffer if she literally had to wait years to recoup her devastating initial losses. The almost instant comfort she derived from her knowledge, following the transfer, that what still constituted the bulk of her life savings was now and forever safe, confirmed the legitimacy of her choice. To just sit tight, no matter what, and think long term might be, all things considered, the best of all possible strategies for the market as a whole. It might be the strategy of choice for the best and the brightest of investors, but it was a terrible strategy for a delicate soul and a chronic worrier like Charlotte.

And therein lies the crux of much of what is wrong with traditional economic theory. Ever since John Stuart Mill there has been an abiding belief that *Homo economicus*—"Economic Man"—is a creature compounded essentially of rationality, self-interest and free will.

Whenever possible, we will make decisions that affect our own best interests as logically and efficiently as we can. It has only been with the rise of the new field of behavioural economics that the idea—known to psychotherapists for at least a century—that people are often irrational, has begun to be even considered.

The MIT economist Dan Ariely is a leader in this burgeoning field. His surprisingly readable, best-selling book *Predictably Irrational* is chockfull of imaginative and highly practical applications of behavioural economics to the vicissitudes of everyday life. His unique way of combining shrewd psychological insights with deceptively simple but ingenious economic experiments intuitively rings true. He makes the point, over and over again, that human behaviour, despite our best intentions, is often irrational. By irrational, Dan Ariely seems to mean what cognitive scientists mean: whatever falls appreciably short of the gold standard for rational decision-making—efficient maximising of your benefits-over-cost ratio—is irrational. The discovery that continues to rock the world of behavioural economics and is considered so revolutionary is that people, once you scientifically examine their behaviour, turn out to be "predictably irrational".

From our standpoint, the cognitive psychologist and behavioural economist are making two critical, unexamined assumptions here, both of which are unsubstantiated: (1) that whenever possible, we *should* make decisions like computers do; and (2) that we *can*, at our best, make such decisions. From our standpoint, once you use the real time model of how people behave—how they make decisions in the real world—an intriguingly different picture emerges. Yes, people are often irrational, but not in the same way, and not for the same reasons, as when judged against the computational standards of an impersonal computer. Yes, goals are pursued and decisions are made, but often unconsciously. And never as therapists do we see people who announce, as their presenting problem, that they wish to maximise their benefit/cost ratio *vis-à-vis* some pressing problem. Even the professionals, or especially the professionals whom we see in therapy—financial advisors, stockbroker analysts, computer experts—do not do this. It was instructive during the current stock-market crash and when the bubble burst at the end of the 1990s, how little these experts were motivated by the traditional economic model, how quickly they gave way to panic, and how much more was at stake than the health of their portfolios.

In what follows, I show how much more complex so-called irrational behaviour looks when viewed from a psychodynamic standpoint.

It's all relative

Somewhere in the beginning of his book, Dan Ariely challenges the reader to "think quick": which would you choose—a ten-dollar free gift certificate or a twenty-dollar free gift certificate for which you first have to pay seven dollars? If you chose the free ten-dollar certificate, you did what most people do. You also chose irrationally, according to Dan Ariely. Irrationally because a moment's thought shows that thirteen dollars (twenty minus seven) is a better deal than ten dollars. Irrational, because all things being equal, it is mathematically impossible that thirteen is not greater than ten.

But all things are not equal between the two choices. From a psychodynamic standpoint, there is a considerable difference between being offered something for nothing and being asked to first put up seven dollars in order to get something presumably greater down the road. For suddenly, the element of risk has entered the picture. How do you know, if you pay the seven dollars, you will receive the free twenty-dollar gift certificate? Or that, if you do receive the twenty-dollar gift certificate, it will prove to have been worth the trouble to write the cheque, the waiting period that is entailed, and the effort you must now make to at last redeem your investment? Whereas, by contrast, if you accept the free ten-dollar certificate, there is nothing to do. If you're not up to redeeming it, or if there's nothing particular you want to buy, you don't have to. In one state, you are as passive and free as you want to be; in the other, you are required to act.

Or consider this: you are looking at an ad featuring three different vacation sites, at three luxurious hotels, at roughly the same rates. First is a trip to Paris. Second is a trip to Paris, but minus the free breakfast. Third is a trip to Rome. Which do you choose? Overwhelmingly, people choose the first hotel, the trip to Paris, which happens to include a free breakfast. This, according to Dan Ariely, is exactly the one the marketers and designers of the ad wanted you to choose, the other two hotels in this example serving merely as "decoys". Decoys, because marketers already know that when consumers do comparison shopping, they typically like to start with easy comparisons. So they slyly insert two other hotels—the Paris hotel without the free breakfast, and the nondescript hotel in Rome—to create an allure of comparison that is really bogus. Bogus because the three hotels all have similar decors and trappings, with the only distinguishing feature being the free breakfast in the first Paris hotel. Because you are unconsciously tempted to make the only easy comparison available—that, all other things being equal, a hotel in Paris which offers a free breakfast is preferable to a hotel in Paris which does not—you wind up purchasing the vacation plan that the marketer all along wanted you to buy. And that, according to Dan Ariely—to purchase an expensive vacation at a Paris hotel, on the basis of a free breakfast—is nothing if not irrational!

Irrational, that is, provided we look at the transaction solely from the insider perspective of the economist, the accountant or the book-keeper. But what about the perspective of the ordinary person in the real world, to whom the prospect of a vacation in a Paris hotel with a free breakfast—if that is all he or she really knows—may sound pretty appealing? Remember we cannot assume that the consumer knows what Dan Ariely and the marketer knows, that there is a joker (the decoy) in the ad. The consumer is right to start out with good faith, to begin by trusting that the ad means what it says, that the three featured hotels, although different, are roughly equal in value, equally deserving of trust, and she has only to exercise her subjective preference. She is right to assume she is not being set up with a decoy. She is right to start with an easy comparison—should she start with a comparison that is too difficult to make? If this is true, what is it then that the comparison is telling her? Viewed from a psychodynamic standpoint, it may tell her, perhaps, that the reason the first Paris hotel is offering a free breakfast is because it tries harder, it is more service-minded and more eager to please. It may tell her the reason the second hotel in Paris is not offering a free breakfast is because it is greedier. Or the reason the hotel in Rome is offering nothing for free is because it is not up to snuff and cannot compete with the others. Or it may tell her none of these things. It may be that the first hotel is offering a free breakfast because it is less successful, attracts fewer tourists, and needs a gimmick. It may be that food in Paris is cheaper than in Rome and therefore easier to give away. While any or all of these scenarios may be equally plausible, the fact is that the ad provides specific information, gives a concrete example that applies only to the first Paris hotel, the vacation plan it is aiming to sell. The marketer, with the help of a covert manipulation, lulls the consumer into falling for an easy comparison. Is it naive or irrational for a consumer to respond this way? Only if you expect that the consumer should somehow have figured out that—beneath the bland appearance of the ad—a deft marketing con game was afoot. But if you grant the consumer the right, as I do, to assume the ad is in good faith, until proven otherwise, you have every reason to initially believe that the offer of a free breakfast may indicate the possibility of a better deal.

Anchoring

Behavioural economists such as Dan Ariely are struck with the power of first impressions when it comes to price-setting. They note that, "although initial prices are 'arbitrary', once those prices are established in our minds they will shape not only present prices but also future ones". This makes them "coherent". It is also what makes them an economic anchor. It is why Dan Ariely likens the power of initial prices to endure to the power of *imprinting*: Konrad Lorenz's celebrated discovery that goslings, soon after their birth, become attached to the first moving object they encounter. If that irresistible object turns out to be a human being—as it was in a very famous experiment in which Konrad Lorenz substituted *himself* for the goslings' mother—they will proceed to loyally follow him throughout much of their lives. With characteristic boldness, Dan Ariely poses the question: Could the human brain, therefore, be "wired like that of a gosling?"

The therapist, unlike the behavioural economist, does not dwell on the pivotal decision impelling a person to purchase an object. The therapist picks up the story—the story of the person's relationship to the object—where the economist leaves off, which is usually at the beginning. For the economist, once the buyer's remorse has been successfully overcome, the story ends. But the therapist knows what it is like for a person to live for a very long time with a product, to be surrounded by them, possessed by them, to identify with them, to dream about them.

Behavioural economists, by contrast, seem intoxicated with the allure of the first impression. They underestimate the power of the unconscious to *select* the first impression. They forget that a hundred different people exposed to the same situation will have a hundred at least slightly different first impressions. If this is so, the question becomes why does a person select—out of thousands of possible descriptions—just one? And a psychodynamic answer might be that certain unconscious characterological traits—either aroused or threatened by the novelty of the encounter—are stimulated to register their vote: approach or withdraw. In this sense, to expect each succeeding impression to supersede or correct the first impression would be like expecting each succeeding time you watched a particular movie or heard a song to somehow come across as a different experience.

Traditionally, the mantra of the marketer has been that people are a federation of stimulus and response hot buttons that in themselves can be arbitrary and meaningless. It has been the innovation of behavioural economists like Dan Ariely to add for the first time a pinch of common-sense folk psychology to the mix. As he points out, not all first impressions endure, some are changeable. From the psychodynamic point of view, this is because all first impressions can be subdivided into a combination of primary and superficial qualities. Primary qualities would tend to be more chemical; how, for example, you rated someone or something on the beauty to ugliness continuum; would involve fundamental needs such as the need to feel safe with another person; or basic values, such as whether instinctively you admire someone or not; or issues of self-esteem (such as does the person make you feel worthy or not); or characteristics such as the degree of genuine likability, apparent warmth; attentiveness to your inner self; compatibility and so on.

One of the biggest reasons our initial impression of others changes is simply because people are so complex they could not possibly, even if they wanted to, reveal all of their salient personality traits in one fell swoop. And, in point of fact, they go to considerable lengths to mask what they consider their least attractive and most negative traits: typically, their capacity for rage, for mean-spiritedness, for envy, for untrustworthiness and so on. Viewed this way, we immediately see one obvious reason why first impressions tend to last: they are based on those qualities in a person that we think are least likely to change.

Arousal

Imagine being an eighteen-year-old male, heterosexual Berkeley student responding to a campus ad seeking participants for a study on "decision-making and arousal". You are told the experimental sessions would require about an hour of your time, for which you would be paid ten dollars a session, and that the sessions would involve sexually arousing material. Questions would be delivered through a specially coded computer. One set of questions would deal with sexual preferences: Do you find women's shoes erotic? Could you imagine being attracted to a fifty-year-old woman? Could you enjoy having sex with someone you hated? Could you enjoy being tied up or tying someone up? A second set of questions would ask about the likelihood of engaging in immoral behaviour such as date rape. A third set of questions would ask about the likelihood of engaging in behaviour related to unsafe sex.

That was the first part of the experiment, supposedly conducted in a cold, dispassionate state. In a second, critical part of the same experiment, conducted a few days later, test subjects were to meet with the same experimenter. Although the questions would be essentially the same as before, you were asked to sign a consent form. This time, you were to get yourself into an excited state by viewing a set of arousing pictures (on the computer) and masturbating. You were to arouse yourself to a high level, but not to ejaculate. At which point, you were to answer the questions.

No one I think will be surprised that the answers given in the aroused state were significantly more permissive, libertine, and daring when it came to conventional taboos. Based on these results, which were consistently arrived at, Dan Ariely concludes that people—people in general, not just 18-year-olds—tend to be poor prognosticators when in a dispassionate state, of what their sexual behaviour would be when they were aroused.

From the psychodynamic standpoint, needless to say, such a conclusion is hardly warranted. Dan Ariely is assuming that the answers given in the second experimental session, with the subjects at peak arousal, are a better indicator of what they would do if faced with the actual situation. He does not seem to consider that his very excited subjects—who, after all, will face no consequences for whatever deviant behaviour they happen to be contemplating—may be *seriously overestimating* what they would really do in circumstances in which they would be held strictly accountable. The fact that there is a significant difference between the two sets of answers does not tell you what the difference means. Dan Ariely is putting an awful lot of faith in the reliability of eighteen-year-old college students who are trying to earn ten dollars for an experimental session with a computer and perhaps to have a little fun along the way.

Here then is a different psychodynamic explanation that suggests itself. It may be that cold, dispassionate, unaroused students are motivated to *underestimate or deliberately play down* what they might do if aroused. After all, does it make sense to be totally frank, to reveal everything to a total stranger in an even stranger test? Conversely, isn't it understandable that someone, when genuinely aroused—as, for example, when intoxicated—or when nearly orgasmic—would be inclined to be more reckless? Such a person may be simply giving vent to some long-held libidinous fantasies. Sex with someone I hate? Why not? Turned on by a shoe? Who knows? Engage in bondage games? Might be fun! Such a person may be doing the very opposite of honestly attempting to predict their behaviour in an aroused state.

In short, Dan Ariely, in a fashion characteristic of the behavioural economist, has relied upon a tightly controlled but almost comically contrived situation in order to reach a sweeping generalisation about the behaviour of real people in real time in the real world. Nevertheless, despite that basic psychodynamic reservation, Dan Ariely in *Predictably Irrational* raises a wealth of intriguing questions.

He wonders why, for example, we persistently tend to "overvalue what we have". Struggling to introduce a psychological dimension, he suggests that is because: (a) owning something entails a certain set of experiences and perspectives that make it difficult to imagine what life would be like without it; and (b) we wish to avoid the mourning we believe would be triggered by its loss. Although true to a certain extent, Dan Ariely, like most economists, does not seem to appreciate that the *relationship we have to a product is more important than the price of the product*. That ownership is essentially about experience (which includes the experience of the product's price fluctuations). Like other behavioural economists, he tries to assign numbers to qualia that are essentially experiential, and then use these numbers to construct a putative, bottom-line, determinative database. Needless to say, from a psychodynamic point of view, the resulting equation between a person's experiential qualia and numbers arbitrarily assigned by an economist—like the proverbial comparing of apples and oranges—does not hold up.

To economists such as Dan Ariely, however, it makes sense to trade in what we have, if what we have has outlived its usefulness or if we can get something comparable at a better value. Not to do so, is simply irrational, a failure to understand or to deal with the cynical realities of the marketplace. Here in a nutshell is the mindset of the economist: ownership is about value; value is about benefits; benefits are about quantitative units. From such a point of view, to appraise a person's possessions is not unlike appraising their portfolio. But this is to disregard the manifold array of different meanings that owning something can convey. It overlooks that *personal identity* is often inextricably bound up with ownership. That ownership can convey a sense of potency, of social standing, of competency, of achievement, of having roots, of good fortune, of all-around desirability, of erotic magnetism. That, conversely, loss of ownership can convey a diminution of power, of the ability to defend and hold on to what is rightfully yours, a costly failure to keep up with the changing times, a sign of surrender, a retreat from the battlefield of life.

Why dealing with cash makes us more honest

In an intriguing chapter, Dan Ariely asks if we think the architects of Enron's collapse would have "stolen money from the purse of an old woman?" He further notes, while they may have literally bilked millions of dollars in pension monies from countless numbers of old women, they would have found it unthinkable to "hit a woman with a blackjack and pulled the cash from her fingers". He concludes it is considerably easier to cheat if it doesn't directly involve cash or money, and surmises that our code of honour (what psychologists call our superego) essentially applies to personal relations with people and not to anonymous tokens or symbols of money one or two removes away from the real thing. (Thus, it is incredibly tempting to heist a featureless pencil or two from a faceless corporation that—you can rationalise— could not care less).

Here, as elsewhere, Dan Ariely shows clever insights into everyday human behaviour. But he wants to have it both ways. He wants to recognise and to accept—as against the traditional concept of *Homo economicus*—that when it comes to economic decision-making we are "predictably irrational", but he wants to maintain that such behavioural economic irrationality can and should be made more rational. Such behaviour, from this point of view, may be due to faulty wiring in the brain or cognitive deficits of reasoning which conspire to create the economic equivalent—when it comes to rational decision-making—of an optical illusion: we think we are logically and efficiently maximising our benefits when we are only being patently irrational.

Nowhere does it seem to occur to the behavioural economist that such cognitive misfirings (which certainly are a factor) may also indicate a general failure of cognitive neuroscience to include the psychodynamic approach for a more comprehensive understanding of the range of dynamic unconscious triggers that are involved.

Thus, the behavioural economist, in yet another variation of their favourite theme, considers the woman who is quite happy to discover a one dollar bill lying in the street, but conversely disappointed if simultaneously her friend, who is walking with her, happens to find a twenty dollar bill—to be unquestionably irrational. Yet, what could be more understandable from a psychodynamic point of view? The difference between being the lucky recipient of a free dollar bill and the person who easily could have but didn't find a nearby twenty dollar bill—have you ever discovered a twenty dollar bill lying in the street in your life?—is huge. For the simple addition of one other person, albeit a friend, or especially a friend, immediately opens a Pandora's box of troubling questions and feelings. Is the friend, for example, going to or should the friend at least offer to share some of the twenty dollars which certainly could have been found by the other? Did the friend spy the twenty dollars well in advance of her announcing she had found it, in other words did the friend covertly try to steer her companion or shield her view from the serendipitous gift? Is her friend inwardly gloating at her luck? Was it obtuseness perhaps on the part of the woman not to have spied the twenty dollar bill? Was her discovery of a paltry dollar bill in fact one more quotidian confirmation of her status as just another loser?

Such questions, which never seem to occur to the behavioural economist, immediately spring from the psychodynamic mindset. To the therapist who daily delves into the interior minds of patients, fantasies of sibling rivalry, of being unfairly passed over, of losing one's rightful place because of some quirk of fate, are, if not universal, hardly uncommon. We hear time and again from patients the haunting, bitter refrain, "If only …". If only they had realised much earlier how precarious the relationship—they could have sworn it was rock solid—really was. If only they had not made that one terrible mistake, how different their lives might have turned out. If only their mother … their father … or their sister had truly loved them. Long ago, in *The Psychopathology of Everyday Life*, Freud pointed out that our sense of free will can be attributed, to a great extent, to our ignorance of our own unconscious. Our actions, upon analysis, he famously said, are not the product of a one-to-one cause and effect relationship—they are *overdetermined*.

Most of these critical psychic determinants, however, are unconscious and—because the person tends to be aware only of what is subject to conscious control—he or she often has the illusion of almost unlimited free will.

We immediately see from this perspective how compelling the fantasy of the "near miss"—for example, if I had been walking ten feet closer to that twenty-dollar bill in the street—can be. In our culture, there may be no better example of its addictive power than prime-time sports (I am writing this in the midst of the 2008 World Series which, almost by definition, is a "game of inches").

This difference between the cognitive and the psychodynamic can be applied to every single example, no matter how trivial, that the behavioural economist raises. Thus, Dan Ariely, pointing out that people don't really know what they want, mentions the hot new networking trend, speed-dating. In a single evening, by spending just a couple of minutes with each prospect, you can canvas an entire room. By comparing stated preferences prior to such an experience with the actual behaviour exhibited, studies reveal a surprising discrepancy between what people say they want in a prospective date, and what they eventually settle for. Illustrative of this, according to Dan Ariely, is the woman who claimed she liked only tall men, who walked into a room full of short men. Did she walk out? Not only did she stay for the entire evening, but she found the experience unexpectedly satisfying.

In other words, she adjusted. Hardly surprising from a psychodynamic point of view. It was Darwin who showed how evolution proceeds by fortuitous adaptation, and how adaptation in turn relies on co-opting—making do with whatever lies at hand. When the context changes, the landscape of adaptive opportunities changes with it. Sitting in a lonely room filling out a questionnaire about the characteristics of Mr. Right—a chance to build your own field of dreams—is a profoundly different experience from wandering into a real room filled with real people. The strategies that are used to solve life problems—unlike the inflexible computer software—are *ad hoc*. Your heart is set on marrying a tall, handsome man? Well, nobody is asking you to marry anybody in the room. This is speed-dating, remember? You're only spending at most a minute or two per man. That's hardly an investment. Why not have fun? Or treat it as just an experiment, a practice session, a dry run for the real thing. After all, people want a lot more than just making decisions that maximise their benefits. They do seek benefits, but not necessarily efficiently computational or quantitative ones. They may instead be emotional, biochemical, or biological benefits that simply contribute to their short-term, but necessary homeostatic comfort rather than to their forward achieving, maximisation of assets. A person may, for example, just want to play, or to be excited, or stimulated. He or she may be in a mood to defy their fears, to be impractical, to be spontaneous, to test their courage.

We see from this point of view that the room full of short men could have presented itself as a challenge to the woman who thought she loved only tall men. As this example shows, it is not just that how people feel about long-term goals can change literally by the hour, but that as their mood changes along with the context, their goals can change too. Nothing is more common than the person who, tired from wrestling with complicated, long-term benefits, surrenders to an irresistible urge for short-term stimulation.

Think how difficult it really is to concentrate steadily on a really important long-term goal—such as studying for a critical exam—how great the temptation is to switch to something, anything more diverting, and less weighty. We can only do heavy lifting for so long; we forget there are few people who like or find mathematics useful in solving life's problems.

The great shortcoming in "behavioural economics" is that it often does not sufficiently distinguish the model it is using—typically a simple, game-like structure with precise moves—from the thing it is modelling. It does not pay enough attention to the fact that the rules we live by in the real world are not nearly so defined or enforceable as those in a virtual game. That there is hardly a consensus in the real world—as there is at the start of every friendly game—as to the rules that are agreed upon and will be adhered to. By way of contrast, in the marketplace of real life where there is inevitably a dynamic conflict of interests—it is the rules that have to be worked out and constantly revised (in reaction to the changing circumstances and shifting strategies of our adversary or whatever is opposing us).

So, yes, behavioural economists are right that people do not know in advance what they want. They are wrong, however, to think what they want is a fixed quantity, an X; and that the road to economic prosperity means finding your X (or your bliss) and then rationally maximising it. People often do not discover what they want—or don't want what they get (hence the cautionary saying "be careful what you pray for").

Viewed psychodynamically, their goals are often unconscious. Unlike professional prognosticators, they are intuitively unwilling to expend more energy in appraising the value of a product than is provided by the immediacy of what economists call a peak experience. In terms of the theory of games, they are less than rigorous. Rather than stay the course, they play *multiple games* that frequently undercut or compete for attention with one another.

This difference between the cognitive and neuroscientific model of behaviour and the psychodynamic model is surprisingly consistent. The cognitive psychologist will look at one variable (cognitive or functional) which is usually interpreted unidimensionally as part of a network of numerous variables. Typically, the experimental subject is presented with a task, a challenge or a puzzle and appraised as to how well he or she resolves it. The underlying assumption is that people go through life setting themselves goals or trying to master obstacles or distractions presented by their immediate environment. This, of course, is a picture of how people behave at their jobs and it cannot help but resonate with memories of our early schooling: that critical period wherein great emphasis was placed on the mastery of specific cognitive skills deemed necessary to survive in the increasingly high-tech modern world. Yet, how often do we see people living their everyday lives as though they were taking an exam, straining to perform at peak performance, and racing against the clock as they would if they were playing speed-chess? Cognitive scientists, overly impressed by the prevalence of games in contemporary life, have failed to realise how much of living is *not* a game.

Mental glitches

In recent decades, cognitive psychologists like Steven Pinker and social scientists like Michael Shermer have increasingly embraced the new field of evolutionary psychology, founded by John Tooby and Leda Cosmides. Evolutionary psychology is the attempt to marry the field of evolutionary biology with the tools of cognitive science using the computational theory of the mind as the conceptual bridge. The computational theory of the mind sees both the body and the mind as engaged in an intricate array of information processing tasks—necessary to the survival of our early hominid ancestors—conducted at the neuronal and genomic level. Evolutionary psychologists first search for these ancient "adaptive" solutions, when we were small bands of hunter-gatherers—and then experimentally endeavour to determine where and how they fit in or do not apply to our super high-tech, urbanised style of contemporary living.

Thus, Michael Shermer, a leading social scientist, in his latest book *The Mind of the Market*, tries to explain the fluctuation of the contemporary market by using principles of evolutionary psychology. Markets, he suggests, prosper when they meet the adaptive needs of its participants in an orderly, logical way. They fail when irrationality holds sway. Like most behavioural economists, Michael Shermer attributes irrational decision-making to glitches in our cognitive machinery. These glitches are called *cognitive biases* and what follows are some of the more important ones.

Self-serving bias

We tend to see ourselves, says Michael Shermer, in a "more positive light than others see us". Surveys show most business people, for example, believe "they are more moral" than other business people. Psychologists who study moral intuition think they themselves are more moral "than other psychologists". Michael Shermer notes that in one College Entrance Examination Board survey of 829,000 high-school seniors, "60 percent put themselves in the top 10 percent in ability to get along with others", while there was "0 percent (not one)" who rated themselves average!

I admit, when I first heard this, it sounded impressive, but after a moment's thought a very simple and completely different explanation presented itself. The 829,000 high school seniors who unanimously rated themselves above average in the ability to get along with others—far from conscientiously trying to arrive at the most objective self-appraisal—were hoping to provide the answer they thought most likely to get them into college! In the same fashion as the person being subjected to voir dire in a jury selection will invariably answer "no"—when queried as to whether he or she may harbor racial prejudices—when a more honest answer for just about everyone, at least some of the time, would be "occasionally". Viewed this way, it is entirely improbable that anyone who is applying for an important advancement in life (admission to college or acceptance at an exciting job) would voluntarily rate themselves as sub-par (below average), in any meaningful category.

Introspection bias

We trust our own intuition, not others. Our own introspection, claims Michael Shermer, is the "gold standard", while others are suspect. From the psychodynamic point of view, I can only say, what is supposed to be irrational about that? The only introspective data we are privy to is our direct experience of our own private stream of consciousness. As philosophers are forever reminding us, it is only and always an inference that other people have minds, subjective impressions, sensations and feelings. Compare, for example, the immediacy of our own impression of eating a delicious meal in a restaurant with our impression, should we happen to glance at the neighbour on our right who is eating a similar dish. Is there any comparison? Don't we have access to tens of thousands of sensations that the other cannot have (not being us) and vice versa? Isn't direct, concentrated experience a far better guide to reality than a fleeting, second-hand, passive perception, thought or an inference communicated to us by an entirely different, relatively unknown person? How much easier is it, for example, to believe that our own parents have cared for us rather than the parents (whom we may never have seen) of some acquaintance? The closest we come to believing we have a direct pipeline to another's feelings (although we still can't) is when we perceive the person to be in undeniable pain. As Wittgenstein famously noted of the nearby person—who is crying out in pain—"try not to believe that". And, of course, looked at from the standpoint of evolutionary psychology, when we were hunter-gatherers, and group cohesiveness and loyalty to the tribe were lynchpins of our survival— when we literally could not survive without the aid of others—the ability to instinctively empathise with a visibly distressed neighbour would be invaluable.

Such immediate, visceral empathy, however, does not generally come into play in the kind of detached, cognitive decision-making that is prevalent in today's decidedly anti-hunter-gatherer world. It makes sense, therefore, to treasure our own introspection, feelings and needs above all others. To act, as Steven Pinker incisively puts it, as though "this spot of earth I am standing on is the most special in the world". This, of course, is to behave egocentrically. This is to say, as Freud long ago pointed out, that human beings are inherently narcissistic (in both a healthy and unhealthy way). From such a human-all-too-human perspective, it makes sense that we tend to overvalue our own accomplishments and undervalue those of others. It makes sense that we are confident when critiquing others—*we don't suffer the consequences of their shortcomings*—but we suffer terribly from our own!

Confirmation bias

This is the almost universal trait of not only preferring to be right rather than wrong but of actively if unconsciously looking for evidence that seems to corroborate our beliefs. It sounds suspiciously like the classic psychoanalytic defence mechanism of rationalisation that has been around almost a century, and it resonates with the equally fundamental psychodynamic idea that all thinking is to a certain extent motivated: that is, in the service of basic emotional, survival needs. It points to a curious split or ambivalence in evolutionary psychology: it wants its cake and to eat it, too. It wants to be rooted in evolutionary biology—in the anthropological study of our most primitive, instinctual, survival-driven needs—and it wants the precision and cachet of a neuroscientific theory predicated on a computer-driven, modular model.

Because cognitive neuroscience relies so heavily on a computer model, it often tries to solve complex psychological puzzles by translating them into tasks that an android or robot might solve. It forgets that what drives the quest for specific computational solutions is the motivation to serve some pressing, biologically rooted, emotional need. By way of contrast, think of *Deep Blue*, IBM's chess-playing computer, at the moment of its historic triumph over the then world-reigning chess champion, Gary Kasparov. Imagine, if you can, what it would be like to have actually achieved something that unprecedented. Then imagine a machine, of unparalleled computing power, yet one that has never had a single experience, feeling, thought, daydream, reflection, question, doubt, perception or emotion. A machine that has never been conscious or unconscious. That does not, for example, know the meaning of the word existence. The name of the planet on which it resides. The definition of a chess game. The difference between a human being and a Swiss knife. That has no fear of death. Has never had an original thought. That wants nothing for itself, that does not know the meaning of wanting, that is as indifferent to winning as to losing.

From this standpoint, we see there is more than computing skills when it comes to grappling with life's problems. Regarding the confirmation bias we are therefore right to trust our own perceptions over that of others. We are right to trust what we know about the past over what we can predict about the future. We are right to trust what we have experienced and observed, what has been tested, has proved solid and dependable, what we can feel in our bones—over some shadowy, abstract idea of some other mind or minds that may or may not be superior to ours, that we are not even sure exists. It makes sense, in short, to put our faith, within reason, in the world that we know best—not the world of the computer or fMRI machine—but the world of our private experience.

The ultimatum game

Imagine this: you are given a hundred dollars with the only stipulation that you are to split it up in any way you see fit with a designated partner. Your game partner, who has no say in how the money should be divided, can either accept or reject the offer. If your partner accepts, you are both instantly richer by the amount of the split. Given these conditions, how much should you offer, how much should you accept? If you are the decider, should you keep as much as ninety dollars for yourself? And conversely, if you are the designated partner, should you accept as little as ten dollars for yourself? According to standard economic theory, *Homo economicus*, a rationally self-maximising creature, should offer as little as possible to the game partner. To do otherwise is what behavioural economists like Dan Ariely call "predictably irrational". And what evolutionary psychologists like Michael Shermer call "reciprocal altruism"—you scratch my back, I'll scratch yours (Shermer, 2011, p. 247).

Reciprocal altruism is a supposedly adaptive trait formed by evolution in our ancestral past, which enhances social cohesiveness by fostering a necessary sense of fair play. In a supposedly amazing result, the ultimate game—played worldwide online much like that of the runaway trolley car and similarly exhaustively studied—decisively refutes the prediction made by the standard economic theory. The most popular offer, the one that is consistent across many countries, is seventy–thirty. Proposals that deviate much beyond the seventy–thirty split, are typically rejected. In other words, splits of eighty–twenty, ninety–ten just "aren't fair". Although such behaviour may make little sense economically, it is supposedly a telling example of what happens when our ancient, evolutionary sense of reciprocal altruism kicks in.

Yet, from the psychodynamic standpoint, it makes all the sense in the world to turn down an offer as paltry as ten dollars. Such a person is making a moral statement, not only about fairness, but about the type of transaction we are willing to invest in. Such a person is saying, in effect, he or she regards an individual whose best offer is an insulting ninety–ten split, as being shamelessly selfish, narcissistic, and blatantly manipulative, using the leverage of being the one calling the shots, in a patently ruthless way. It becomes immediately apparent from that perspective that to accept the ten dollars would be to accept "dirty money". It would be to compromise their values for a meagre sum and to simultaneously gratify an unethically mercenary partner. In this sense, turning down the proposal—far from being simply irrational—would be to send a message how the person *feels about* the proposal and what they are prepared to stand behind. It is a message that alternately could be interpreted as saying: "You may not be fair—but I am!"; or "There are more important things in the world than money"; or "You know what you can do with your split". If, for example, we happen to be late—and someone we truly dislike offers us a ride in their car—is it irrational to turn it down (and thereby incur the unnecessary expense of a train fare)? Is it irrational to be offended if you have been invited to share a cooked dinner and the host takes ninety per cent of the meal (which he prepared) and offers you ten per cent?

The behavioural economist, by placing so much importance on the power of money, overlooks the extent to which meaning and inner fulfilment cannot be quantified. He dismisses the widespread spiritual point of view which often regards evil as the fruit of succumbing to the immediate gratification of cynical short-term pleasures; he downplays the more long-term, hard-won satisfactions purchased by living and acting in a more honorable, necessarily more self-sacrificing, self-denying fashion—directly opposed to a selfishly self-maximising philosophy of *Homo economicus*.

Consider, for example, the evolutionary psychologists' explanation of why people value telling the truth, rather than focusing on being able to cheat without getting caught: it is that if you *know* that you are trustworthy, you are more likely to be convincing than if you know you are lying; and if you are perceived to be trustworthy, you are far more likely to be the beneficiary of the loyalty of the group than if you are reputed to be a cheater. It is worth noting that evolutionary explanations of this kind—which routinely ignore the various psychodynamic benefits that can be derived from a positive relationship with one's self (making for a healthy self-esteem)—instead focus primarily on the available interpersonal social benefits (group relations).

In this respect, it may be that evolutionary psychology, and especially cognitive neuroscience, in their emphasis on the computational theory of the mind, are unconsciously reflecting the ethos of the capitalistic society we live in. By contrast, the psychodynamic view I am proposing, rather than opposing the capitalistic idea of a free world, tries to complement it. It recognises that to be moral requires more than being a law-abiding, trustworthy member in one's community, a good Samaritan when necessary, a person who does not flout the basic mores of one's society. It recognises that to be rich does not imply that one is moral. To acquire wealth is not to find meaning. As often, it can imply the person is grasping and egocentric.

Behavioural economists get into trouble because they do not acknowledge the contradiction and the challenge—to both evolutionary psychology and cognitive neuroscience—presented by the psychodynamic factor of primary emotion. Instead, they falsely equate cold-blooded rationality with morality, as though the satisfaction of just emotion is somehow irrational. As though the accumulation of monies is more rational, and therefore more moral, than the accumulation of positive feelings of genuine self-esteem.

Behavioural economists, social scientists and evolutionary psychologists like Michael Shermer (who can be all of these things) seem to believe that important life decisions can or should be made on the basis of a rational, decision-making computer in which the complexity of real life can be translated into a quantitative cost and benefit analysis. Because of this bias, cognitive science makes the following fallacious assumptions, none of which have ever been proved: that a method exists for redescribing and operationalising the manifold aspects of whatever it is that is meaningful, self-fulfilling, actualising, satisfying, unsatisfying, life-affirming, life-negating, pleasurable, or depriving. That the intrinsic dynamic nature of thought and emotion, of higher cortical functions and the more universal, basic emotions (as conceptualised by evolutionary biology and evolutionary psychology) can somehow be separated and reduced from an ongoing life process to a series of computationally distinct, cognitive tasks. That the infinite array of life's problems, which we daily have to live through, can somehow be systematically addressed and hopefully solved with essentially cognitive tools, without input from our idiosyncratic, affective histories.

To his credit, Michael Shermer, in his book *The Mind of the Market*, does his best to broaden the behavioural economist's narrow definition of what it means to be a self-maximising agent. In an effort to explain the basis for human happiness, for example, he dons his evolutionary psychologist's hat and harkens back to our ancestral roots when we were small primate bands. Our survival, then, he notes, depended on tight social and tribal bonds—*not money*—which is why so often studies confirm that money does not bring happiness. He cites what he refers to as "the lottery test"—if you won the lottery, what would you change about your life? If it is your job (a popular choice of many who take the test), it means you are basically unsatisfied with what you do. Here Shermer brings in evolutionary psychology to fill the economic void, pointing to our deep-rooted ancestral need for tribal bonding. It was religion after all, he says, that preceded statehood, nation-building and large-scale government, and that served to cement the necessary primate social bonds needed for survival and to provide the early leadership and instruction to foster them, which is why so many people say religion means so much to them, and is so essential to their need for consolation during times of tragic loss, when money cannot buy happiness.

We see that Michael Shermer is conflating two historically separate tools—cognitive social neuroscience and evolutionary psychology—to replace psychodynamic explanation. From these dual perspectives, emotions are dealt with as being primarily the coded immediate purveyor of crucial survival information: that is, if a substance tastes bad, it is poisonous; if a feeling of hunger persists, it is time to eat; if you are afraid of something, don't ignore what makes you afraid. For the behavioural economist, only emotions leading to enhanced economic fitness—which by definition means greater survival value—are rational ones. They are quick to dismiss the psychodynamic insight that the relationship a person has to their money is fluid. More like the relationship he or she has to their height, weight and age: as you change, it changes.

Although behavioural economists acknowledge the motivational influence of emotion, they tend to regard emotion more like a necessary evil. They forget that most of us are not heartless businessmen. That it is emotional valence, not logic or rationality, that tells us when we are being mercenary. That much of what we consider most meaningful in life depends on *not* being materialistic. That sometimes values are actually determined by how they stand in contrast to economic ones. That we are generous to the extent we give our money to less fortunate but worthy others. We are prodigal to the degree that we scorn the hoarding of money; we are carefree to the degree we do not obsess on money; ascetic to the extent we transcend materialistic concerns; entrepreneurial to the degree we daringly risk our money; Christian to the degree we spurn the value of money.

It is, in sum, the much richer psychodynamic point of view which includes—in addition to the cognitive and the rational—the human all-too-human vicissitudes of irrationality, temperamentality, the pursuit of existential meaning and acknowledgement of life's unknowable contingencies.

Needless to say, we would expect to find none of these values in a professional economist. Analogous to how a venture capitalist is defined as much, or perhaps more, by the amount of risk he or she is willing to take, as by the ultimate success or failure of their venture, the adventurer or explorer is not defined by the extent to which they maximise their health fitness.

We immediately see why the economic model has traditionally had little to say about the gambling, addictive side of making money, the side that cannot live without endless transfusions of credit, which obsessively links self-esteem to upward mobility, the side that is manifestly irrational. Yet, this is the side, especially in times of financial panic— when there is both greed to make a killing and a desperate attempt to hoard one's savings—that can be a prime target for magical thinking and a host of emotional disorders. The side that needs to be addressed psychodynamically.

It is that integral if ungovernable part of human nature that can foil the best-laid plans of whomever would download our minds onto their favourite computer.

CHAPTER FOUR

One on one with God

As Duane would tell it to me:

> I was sitting in the front row when Mailer came in, and I was surprised by how old he looked. While he was being introduced, for some reason, he started to stare at me. I had no idea why. It made me very uncomfortable. I would've walked out, but it would have been embarrassing.
>
> He gave a pretty good talk on literature and at the end I asked him a question about the *Deer Park*. That interested him, and looking straight at me, he gave a long, thoughtful answer.

Why would anyone, I wondered, much less Norman Mailer, need to bully Duane—a wool-gathering graduate student who never had been involved in a fist fight in his life—who was an aspiring composer closing in on a doctorate in music at Yale and who had nothing but youthful reverence for the brilliant iconoclast? Was it just one more instance of what the writer himself was fond of referring to as "my combative ego"?

It had been the first thing I thought of when I learned that Norman Mailer had died. Maybe because I couldn't believe such a dynamic, larger-than-life figure, who had been more like a force, a Zeitgeist incarnate, had been permanently silenced. Famous at twenty-five, he had been part of our national consciousness for over fifty years. He had boasted, in *Advertisements for Myself*, of "hitting the longest homerun"—in regards to someone finally writing the Great American Novel—that anyone had ever seen. And from the very first time I had encountered Normal Mailer in a television interview, nearly forty years ago, he had struck me as the most articulate intellectual I had ever seen. Even more, he had seemed for a writer the most naturally talented amateur philosopher I had come across.

Although that impression would not change, it was his combativeness—his defiant "I'm the champion until they knock me off" attitude he so admired in his hero, Hemingway—that I would remember. Who could forget Dick Cavett's celebrated comeback to Norman Mailer—who had baited him for having to look to a cue sheet for things to say—"Why don't you take it and fold it five different ways and put it where the moon don't shine!" (Mailer, 2010, pp. 238–239). Or the time he had taken boxing lessons from former light-heavy champion Jose Torres, shadow boxed with Muhammad Ali, or tried his hand as a ringside boxing analyst?

At the time of Mailer's death, I was finishing a new book, *God and Therapy*, that just happened to coincide with his most recent and to my mind most completely unexpected publication, *On God: An Uncommon Conversation*, Normal Mailer, with Michael Lennon. Prior to that, I had been especially intrigued with *The Gospel, According to the Son*, but I could not motivate myself to get past the devastatingly negative reviews, and besides, that was a novel. But this was a conversation and nobody had ever accused Normal Mailer of being less than forthright when asked to give his opinion. Knowing Mailer to be an unforgiving critic of any organised religion and to dabble occasionally in free-ranging metaphysical speculation, I had been taken aback, shortly before his death, to hear him respond, sober as a judge, in a televised interview—upon being asked if he believed in an afterlife—"I believe in reincarnation. Why else are we here?"

So, did Norman Mailer wind up his life really believing in some kind of orthodox God? Had one of the keenest observers of the human condition, one of our most caustic intellects, in the end succumbed to the siren call of religious consolation? That didn't make sense because Mailer had a reputation for being absolutely fearless when it came to standing behind his ideas and letting the chips fall where they may. Mailer's God, I decided, could only be the outcome of some tortuous but honest confrontation with our existential fate as the only animal that knows it's going to die. His God would be his answer—the answer of a brilliant, highly undisciplined but wildly creative mind—to our metaphysical predicament. In terms of our theme, it would represent one of the ways we try to make sense of our place in the cosmos.

On God: An Uncommon Conversation proved to be a rather extraordinary testament not only to the depth of Mailer's religious feelings but to the stunning originality of his vision. A Mailerian God, it turns out, is an existential, artistic God. It is more good than bad. It is *not* all-powerful. We are made in His image, but He needs us as much as we need Him. Although He is our Creator, He does not know the outcome of His creation. We are in effect an artistic creation—one of His greatest. He may not even be the only god. There may be many gods.

Like Mailer, God is a warrior who fights against the Devil. Sometimes, however, He is forced to collaborate with the Devil. Because Mailer can conceive of no antecedent first cause—the first cause must be God. Furthermore, in one of those leaps I just cannot understand—Mailer also believes in karma and reincarnation. We do not, however, harbor any memories of our past lives. A good rebirth is "a reward" for a life well lived, while a lesser life earns a lesser rebirth or, perhaps, no rebirth. Mailer muses that God may allow exhausted or inferior souls to just die without rebirth. And lest he be misunderstood, Mailer reiterates how much he despises every kind of organised religion and all organised governments.

What is remarkable is how passionate and invested Normal Mailer is in these admittedly far-out ideas. Fifty years ago, he was a proud atheist, but now he seems to be winging it, making up his own theology as he goes along. On the one hand, he repeatedly acknowledges to Michael Lennon, an earnest author and professor of English, who seems well informed on broad theological matters—that he is an "amateur" and not qualified as a theologian—on the other hand, he could not be more free-wheeling and improvisational in elaborating his own characteristically idiosyncratic view of religion.

The more I got into *On God* the more Mailer started to sound like a novelist rather than a philosopher. By the time I had finished the book, it was as though I had read "The Gospel According to Mailer". Mailer's God, protestations aside, turns out to be neither kind nor empathic (like Mailer himself, at least at times). Yet, though I had never been comfortable with Mailer's over-the-top, gung-ho personality, his flirtation with gonzo journalism, I could not help but be touched by the obvious sincerity of this posthumously published book. Mailer, it seemed, had come to terms with something, had achieved some kind of genuine inner peace. But what kind of inner peace? It seemed impossible to imagine because in the final analysis, his book came across, at least to me, as a mass of tantalising contradictions. Despite numerous disclaimers, for example, Mailer fails to show the necessary respect and awe for the magnitude of the unknown. It is almost as though he has talked himself into thinking he is capable of glimpsing God's mind. An undeniable, manic, if cheerful, quality pervades *On God*.

Yet, for all these reasons, no one who was not already a believer in reincarnation before reading this, could ever be persuaded by it. Although a great deal of creative brilliance and hard-earned wisdom shine through *On God*, its sole rhetorical trick, it seems to me, is to substitute God and the Devil for everything that is loving, compassionate, wise, creative, and just—and for everything that is malevolent, toxic, evil, jealous, mean-spirited, and cruel—about the world. Not surprisingly, Mailer never feels the need to say why he assumes the existence of divine presences. There are times when, having gathered a head of steam, the author is unembarrassed to boldly speculate on the mind, the intentions, and the conflicts of God, as though he were just another character, albeit a cosmic character, in one of his novels.

Perhaps we can see why the moment before his death—according to one bedside witness—a wide grin crossed his face "as though he had just seen something amazing" (Mailer, 2010, p. 394). In his last act, true to the creative existentialist code by which he had lived his life, Mailer had transformed his final experience into a karmic vision of what the afterlife had in store for him!

In sum, the God of Norman Mailer was many things. An artist. A novelist. An existential improviser. A biological engineer of new worlds. A fallible being. A possessor of superhuman, but limited powers. A restless, passionate Creator. A warrior who fought with the Devil. For me the great psychological question is: did Mailer realise he was simply drawing an elevated portrait of his own demons and better angels writ large? Did he realise that more than any other writer I know, Mailer has included himself, has placed himself dead centre in his own theological system? Was he aware how incredibly novelistic his theological system was? How much its lifelike, chaotic, violent, existential, and totally unpredictable character *resembled his own volatile life*? The extent to which he tries to engage God? Play games with Him? Go one on one with Him? Get God to count on him, admire him, need him, have as open a relationship as possible with him?

It follows the shortcomings in Mailer the theologian will closely mirror the shortcomings in Mailer the man. Mailer does not seem to understand his need to elevate everything about himself to divine status. That he must be either God's soldier or clown, but he can never be (as we all occasionally are) just small-minded, mean-spirited, pompous or boring. He seems unable to acknowledge certain violent impulses in himself that are neither noble nor ignoble—that have nothing to do with either excesses or failures of appropriate existential consciousness-raising—but that can be credited to developmental arrests, characterological disorders and the like. He does not seem able to differentiate between behaviour that is sociopathic, impulse-driven and socially deviant from behaviour that—while fully in the service of the spontaneous creative self—is nevertheless balanced and mature.

Louis Menand, in his wonderful appraisal of Norman Mailer in *American Studies*, notes that no one has ever taken Mailer's philosophy seriously. That may be because Mailer as a philosopher is a daredevil. His obsession with hitting a homerun every time out made him congenitally incapable of that incredible, brick-by-brick, system-building patience that is the hallmark of every genuine philosophic achievement. Menand misses the point, however, when he adds that neither has anyone been interested in Mailer's literary ideas. He overlooks that while Mailer is hardly aspiring to propagate ideas in the manner of an academic, he is dead serious about revolutionising how writers express themselves, which he did, as Menand himself also notes, by more or less inventing (in *The Armies of the Night*) what came to be called the New Journalism. Mailer's discovery was that—by incorporating into his writing actual happenings of unique cultural relevance—the New Journalism could do for non-fiction what the great modernist innovation of the *found object* did for art. It was his inspired innovation to incorporate his own persona—*to make a found object of himself*. And while I was never comfortable with his constant presence, incessant self-advertisement, and outsized ego, there can be no doubt that he gave the New Journalism a possibility of vibrant life it never had before.

So, how did I appraise Norman Mailer's attempt in *On God* to forge a coherent picture of our relationship to whatever transcendental, cosmic forces there may be? First, to his credit, his book, while doggedly theological, is never less than touchingly personal. It is hard not to feel that Mailer, in his guts, is thinking deeply and honestly about his own mortality; yet his mind remains astonishingly alert, philosophical, humorous, and risible. Above all, it is deliciously creative. Mailer has done nothing less than create a religion for only one person, a theology that in no way aspires to converts. It is therefore impossible to penetrate this book, to know to what extent Mailer is trying to fathom the ultimate truth and to what extent he is fearlessly attempting to follow his religious imagination to wherever it will lead him.

I chose this book as an introduction to a pressing modern debate. Can everything religion comprises—the gamut of transcendental, spiritual, moral longings and feelings—ever be fully inscribed in the theological doctrines of a particular religious system? Or can the entire spiritual domain be somehow contained within the explanatory reach of biological science? (That is, can there be such a thing as a God module in the brain?). Into which reductionistic scheme, religion or science, will the cosmos be found? Or are we to look for a possible synthesis instead?

Mailer's contribution, of course, falls in neither camp. If anything, it establishes its own camp, that of the incorrigibly creative, obsessively existential, and stubbornly indefinable. I want to contrast it now with a painfully serious, non-playful, and agonisingly moral rumination on the unknowability of God by a distinguished biblical scholar, Bart Ehrman.

God's problem

This book resonated with me, because it is essentially about what I consider the greatest theological question of all—why do we suffer? It is a question Bart Ehrman has wrestled with for much of his adult life. A question that has preoccupied him in his torturous journey from passionate Christian to equally passionate non-believer. It is a question that can sometimes weigh on his mind in the wee hours of the morning when, as he tells us, he can wake up "in a cold sweat" (Ehrman, 2008, p. 1). It is a question that is movingly encapsulated in the full title of his disturbing book: *God's Problem: How the Bible Fails to Answer Our Most Important Question—Why We Suffer*.

Looking back, from his current emancipated perspective, he does not understand how he could have believed what he believed. Because of the Job-like doubts he had to overcome, his courage in eventually renouncing his faith completely, in some ways seems greater than what is required for the naturally non-believing atheist such as Richard Dawkins, Sam Harris, Daniel Dennett, Carl Sagan or especially Christopher Hitchens. Overall, he comes across as less angry and more compassionate than the typical sceptic. His primary method is to use the Bible to refute the Bible. He does this in large measure through a careful reading of what the various prophets were saying—to whom and in which historical contexts. Along the way, he uncovers many inter-text contradictions and logical absurdities. He shows great ability in taking the reader inside the minds of the prophets and showing how different are the religious questions being addressed today from those during the times the Bible was most likely being written.

By far the bulk of the book, however, is devoted to a rigorous examination of the essential biblical answers to the great question—why is there so much suffering—if a loving, omnipotent, omniscient God, as they tell us, is in charge? Bart Ehrman masterfully lays out the main arguments: God is inflicting suffering on us in order that we may thereby become wiser and stronger; our suffering is coming not from God but from evil people who inflict it on us; and it is a mystery as to why there is such suffering in the world, a mystery we cannot understand on our own but perhaps one day will (with God's help).

Like Harold Kushner before him, Bart Ehrman is devastating in his ability to philosophically expose and ridicule the patent absurdity of such theological arguments. Like Dostoevsky's Ivan in *The Brothers Karamazov*—who cannot accept the suffering of an innocent child and says, "even if such a God exists, I reject him!"—Bart Ehrman cannot accept a God who would torture an innocent child.

It is this combination of obvious biblical scholarship, plus years of devoted service in the ministry, plus manifest good-heartedness and admirable common sense—that seems rooted in this world—that makes him such a compelling witness for a humanist but secular view of the Bible.

He does not discuss conventional arguments for or against God, never mentions evolutionary biology or intelligent design. What he is especially good at is revealing the profound difference in world view between the Old and the New Testament. He shows how primarily (except for the Book of Daniel) the Old Testament prophets did not believe in Heaven, Hell or the afterlife. He shows how Hell, and the Lake of Fire, is to a great extent an apocalyptic invention. How widespread was the belief that the Messiah and the end of the world was imminent. How it was believed that God would come down, revive all the dead, separate the sinners from those who would be saved and dramatically consign the damned—in front of those who would be saved—to the Lake of Fire: that is, Christ: "Some of you shall live to see this"—with those saved ascending to Heaven.

Bart Ehrman notes every apocalyptic since that time (including today) has been wrong in their end of the world prophecy. It was therefore necessary to change the Old Testament's simple *vertical picture of the cosmos* (earth, a below earth, and an above earth) to a *horizontal picture, which for the first time included time* (a here, an afterlife, and a Heaven). The New Testament, concludes Ehrman, did not portray Christ as the Son of God, but as the Son of Man, the prophet of the Messiah and not the Messiah. And finally, the Apocalypse provides one more cause for humanity's suffering: evil represents the temporary earthly triumph of Satan's demons as they battle the forces of good. It will only be on the Day of Judgement when God's angels come down and conquer the demons and those who worship them, consigning them to the Lake of Fire, that evil will be banished from the earth, signalled by the Rapture. This, Ehrman tellingly says, is a theological position perilously close to Manichaeism and dualism, with the implicit admission that God does not completely control the outcome of events.

If Norman Mailer is at the end of a continuum—to find an explanatory system for religious experience—Bart Ehrman is in the middle, and the evolutionary psychologist is at the other end. As a theologian, Norman Mailer is the ultimate Copernican: everything revolves around him. Bart Ehrman is the disillusioned believer: he wants there to be a loving, omnipotent God, but can't find Him. The evolutionary psychologist, who reveres but does not deify the scientific method, dispenses with the need for supernatural consolation and it is to this daring claim we now turn.

Darwin's God

Pascal Boyer is a brilliant anthropologist, who attempts to explain religion by two principal means: evolutionary biology and cognitive psychology. His seminal book, *Religion Explained: The Evolutionary Origins of Religious Thought*, provides a wonderfully logical, explanatory structure of his own highly original point of view. His strategy is to show that religion does not create social situations: it latches on, instead, to already existing, culturally relevant, inference-rich mental systems, and reinforces them. Religion, he ingeniously shows, is therefore *natural* and if it did not exist in a given local culture, most likely it would be invented.

Like most anthropologists, he seems to equate all religions, all tribal and primitive rites (including ours) with one another. The absurd, irrational aspects of religious, magical thinking he explains by alluding to cognitive errors (dissonance, false positive, etc.) and the side effects of our ancestrally rooted evolutionary psychology: that is, the need to think in animistic, coalitional terms. He stresses that, after all, out of countless counterintuitive ideas, only a few will survive: those that meet the numerous needs of already existing, inference-rich systems. All other religious ideas will fall by the wayside.

Whenever he can, Pascal Boyer tries to use the tools of experimental psychology to bolster his theory. He points to certain psychological tests allegedly "proving" that certain supernatural concepts are consistently recalled better than what he calls "mere oddities": that is, citing how "a table that felt sad" was recalled better than "a table made of chocolate" (Boyer, 2001, pp. 51–54). Although this is an interesting observation, I do not find anything, especially from a psychodynamic standpoint, surprising in this result. A table, for example, that really was made out of chocolate could conceivably be found in any New York Chelsea art opening. An actual table, however, that somehow was capable of feeling sad would rock the world of physics. In the same vein, it is hardly surprising that a "man with six fingers" is less remembered than a "man walked through a wall".

What is most impressive about Pascal Boyer is the way he shows there is an underlying cognitive structure to a diversity of supernatural concepts. He mentions, for example, how in a story recall test by J. Barret, the statement, "God saves a man's life and at the same time helps a woman find a lost purse", is remembered as God first helping one person and then attending to the other. Boyer explains this by noting that, from a structural standpoint, supernatural concepts that contain "only one oddity" are recalled better than concepts with two or more oddities. The fact that a manlike God, who is both omnipotent and omniscient, could exist is oddity enough. The fact that such a Supreme Being would also simultaneously be in two different places doing two different things with equal ease and proficiency is too much oddity to handle. Boyer offers this as "proof" that supernatural concepts possess an underlying cognitive structure.

What Boyer cannot say, however, is whether such cognitive structures are the cause or the effect of supernatural concepts. His so-called "proofs" do not really come close to experimentally demonstrating the validity of his theory. Not surprisingly, there is an alternative, and much simpler, psychodynamic interpretation. It is understandable, under the stress of a peculiar story recall, the ordinary person, who cannot be expected to be adept at metaphysical speculation, will have trouble envisioning a rather inconceivable counterintuitive side effect of being omniscient: that is, to be able to be in two seemingly disconnected places simultaneously. They will, instead, unconsciously slip back into a far more familiar form of linear thinking. Does this mean then that they don't really believe in God's omniscience? Or could it mean instead that to believe in God's omniscience requires the same kind of close attention that is needed if one is asked (as they often are in logic tests) to spot the hidden connection between seemingly random, disconnected sentences? That people therefore who believe in God's omniscience, do so analogously in a kind of compartmentalised fashion: a part of their mind believing in a human look-alike who happens to have unlimited powers and another part trying to believe in an unimaginably abstract idea such as infinity, by imagining the simplest and crudest physical object possible (such as counting one object after another without ever coming to an end)?

We see, once again, that evolutionary psychologists like Pascal Boyer seem to forget that they work with toy models of the world, and what they are essentially offering, from a strictly scientific point of view, is an *explanation of their hypothetical toy model*. In no sense can their inferences, once they are applied to the real world from which they have been derived—and on whose behalf they have been co-opted—be said to be specific. If confronted, they will admit this, claiming all they are doing is presenting a first step, albeit exciting and promising, towards a necessarily much fuller explanation.

There can be little doubt their reductive aspirations have been fortified by the spectacular success of their champion, Charles Darwin, who, arguably, managed to reduce the almost infinite diversity of evaluation to the central mechanism of natural selection (a theory that famed cosmologist Roger Penrose has nominated as probably the greatest example of reductive success in the history of the life sciences).

They overlook that natural selection, once hit upon, is incredibly *easy to understand* in the sense that Newtonian gravity—as an instantaneous force in inverse proportion to the squared distance between any two objects (apple and head; moon and ocean tides; human and earth, etc.) can be readily grasped.

They therefore fail to see natural selection, like Newtonian gravity, are classic examples of magically simple algorithms—applicable to an almost infinite diversity of permutations—in no small part because they *do not deal with the emergent* phenomena that can come from group dynamics. Since the most baffling emergent phenomenon in the cosmos is subjective awareness, this means at some point natural selection will get left behind (which is not the same as negating it) and the necessary group dynamics relevant to the particular hierarchical level of emergent complexity will be brought in.

To put it another way, evolutionary psychologists cannot afford the luxury of thinking they are analogous to chess analysts—who actually can explain the infinite diversity of chess positions by always going back to the fundamental, invariant rules of chess. They forget they are not dealing with only one level of explanatory principle—such as chess, arithmetic or geometry—when they attempt (following Darwin) to trace natural selection all the way up to human subjectivity. That they are instead dealing with a multiplicity of emergent phenomena and a diversity of conceptual frameworks. Imagine what it takes, for example, to learn particle physics. Then think of what is entailed in order to master cosmic evolution. To traverse across a span of billions of years, from clouds of gas to organic matter; from cell biology to organic chemistry; to physiology; to neurology; to anthropology; to psychology. Viewed this way, how can evolutionary psychologists be sure they know the fundamental principles by which we evolved from our primitive ancestors to our present heights of subjective awareness? How do they know there may not be numerous levels of emergent phenomena, yet to be discovered, each requiring its own hierarchical conceptualisation? It is one of the great merits of the psychodynamic approach that its *fundamental orientation, from the outset, is interdisciplinary.*

Pascal Boyer, however, hardly makes use of this psychodynamic element. He dismisses, for example, outright the prevailing insight that the primary function of religion is to offer consolation for life's inevitable tragedies. He notes instead that we live in the most affluent, the most comfortable age ever, yet religion continues to be widespread.

That contemporary man does not believe in God or the afterlife in the same sense that a medieval person did, when one would no more question the existence of God than one would question the existence of a mountain or the sky.

It is here, as I point out (in *God and Therapy*) that Pascal Boyer misses the psychodynamic point. It is *because* of the undeniably attenuated belief in the afterlife, that the existential dread of death, and possible non-existence, is so much greater than it was, for example, in medieval times. And that alone can explain much of our need for religion of some kind, even if it is religion on an as-needed basis. We may be more affluent than at any time in history, but—as any psychotherapist can attest—we are prone to great feelings of helplessness. As cognitive psychologists often do, Boyer underestimates just how profound and widespread mental illness is; how modern high-tech medicine— as Elizabeth Kübler Ross famously said—is predicated on an obsessive *denial of death*, rendering us all the more vulnerable when it does come.

Pascal Boyer, in short, is searching for an egalitarian, foundational principle that can explain all religion. He has selected, as his three cornerstones, evolutionary psychology, experimental psychology, and cognitive neuroscience. His unit of cultural transmission is our cognitive machinery. To achieve this, it is necessary to minimise the obvious and profound differences in degree of sophistication between Western religion and almost all other primitive religions. That difference—not only in the quality of its literature but in the subtlety of its theology—seems to me to be as vast as the difference between Western physics and, as Boyer points out, the intuitive physics which all people share.

There are other differences. You would never know, for example, from Pascal Boyer's admittedly wonderful, comprehensive treatment of the roots of religious phenomena—that there was such a thing as a dynamic unconscious, a psychodynamic approach, a concept of a primary process and a secondary one. You might think that the last word on the mind is that of the (very recently arrived) evolutionary psychologist. Or that the idea of modularity in the brain and the model of computational, information-processing, and problem-solving is universally accepted and essentially uncontroversial. Which is hardly the case.

By contrast, what the psychodynamic method offers could not be more different from that of the computer model. It encompasses both the cognitive and evolutionary approaches. It does not exclude the experimental method nor does it avoid quantitative evaluation, but it does not rely solely on it. It does not present a toy model of reality and then struggle to prove that it is similar in principle to the real world. It recognises that you cannot posit an arbitrary, one-dimensional, artificial model based on a game-like situation—prove some underlying, dynamic principle which seemingly illuminates the structure of the set-up—and then claim you have thereby proved the same thing about the realistic situation it supposedly mirrors. (But which is immeasurably more messy, open-ended, uncontrollable and, especially, multidimensional).

It follows, the psychodynamic method will not try to explain almost everything with just one or two disciplines. For example, Pascal Boyer explains the long sought-after unit of cultural transmission of religious concepts with the single idea of what he terms *cognitive relevance*. This is the ability of certain kinds of supernatural concepts to most easily and efficiently tap into basic evolutionary needs. What Boyer means is that supernatural concepts are unconsciously selected in order to satisfy what we imagine we need to survive. Thus, those entities or beings elected to play a supernatural role in our lives invariably, according to Boyer, tend to be "full strategic agents. If some information is strategic to your inference systems, they have access to it". In other words, if you live in a culture where your survival depends on knowing who are your friends and who are your enemies, you can be sure that the supernatural beings (or agents) in your particular religion will know everything there is to know about the subject. Boyer goes on to add: "Such agents are so much easier to represent and so much richer in possible inferences that they enjoy a great advantage in cultural transmission". He notes, by way of counterexample: thus the idea of a "divine brute", a god that is a useless know-nothing, "has little religious future".

Pascal Boyer is so ingenious and judicious in his exhaustive cognitive analysis of the roots of religion that it is hard to disagree with anything he says at a certain level. It is not what he says that is the problem so much as what he does not say. It is hard to imagine that his masterful account—which has undeniable appeal for the anthropologist, evolutionary psychologist and clinical psychologist—would resonate with the non-professional but earnest lay person (the typical religious candidate) who is trying to make sense of his or her place in the cosmos. Take, for example, Boyer's concept of *decoupling*: the ability of human beings from early age on to separate imagining the consequences of an intended action from the need to enact it (accounting, according to

Boyer, for the widespread phenomenon of "the imaginary companion" in children). It is this ability to decouple two things which normally belong together that allows such ideas—as that of supernatural agents watching us—to be recruited over and over again.

Before religion, according to Pascal Boyer, there are complicated, evolved social systems. Religion, which is parasitical, attaches itself to inference systems of the mind which explain sudden misfortune and are based on the existing social or change system with its distinctive strategies for cheater detection and cooperation. The supernatural agents that come to be believed in, will have full access to all the strategic information. Moral intuitions therefore come first and will precede religious values. Boyer gives as an example the prevalence of witches and persons with the evil eye: they are supernatural projections of the paranoid fear that there are certain people who deeply envy what you have and, unless they are thwarted, will put all of their energy into cheating and stealing something from you. The unstated cognitive inference system assumes the gods have a personal relationship. They care about what their supplicants do or don't do and react accordingly: if, for example, there are insufficient sacrifices the god may well send a famine. It is important, says Boyer, that people, including religious leaders, do not seem to mind how such supernatural powers are used—they are deliberately "foggy" on that score—only that the particular gods care enough to become involved.

Building on these cognitive insights, Boyer goes on to ask—why then rituals? His answer—because they are "social gadgets"—constructions which combine a number of innate inference systems, some of which are related to religion and some of which are not. So if religious rituals are "add-ons"—(the presence of supernatural agents at especially sacred religious ceremonies being fairly commonplace)—they are thereby that much more compelling. Thus, rituals can serve as initiation rites (with or without God being present). But if He is present—for example, at a marriage ceremony in the West, with God as your witness—then it is that much more powerful.

Pascal Boyer, therefore, does not find the enduring presence of rituals to be mysterious. They tend to be based on what he terms "naive sociology". They are meant to address the explanatory gap in people's understanding of why rituals seem to create manifest, transformative change. Their answer is that they add agency. They accept this answer, says Boyer, because they do not understand that their mental inference system is really based on evolutionary psychology; that a major change in social status such as marriage has a lasting effect on the social exchange system and therefore needs the coordination of all members to be there at the same time in order to ratify it. The purpose of the wedding ritual is to make this necessary social change salient and easily memorable. Not understanding this, people tend to think that the magical-seeming transformative effect they see stems from the ritual itself. They do not see, says Boyer, that it is the need for salience that creates the add-on of ritual (the ritual, in his view, being the effect, not the cause, of an underlying, social and evolutionary strategy).

At this point, I cannot help noting how much Pascal Boyer sounds like the great sociologist, Erving Goffman, who would explain the most meaningful patterns of behaviour as the manifestation of unconscious social strategies. To me, the flaw in Pascal Boyer's thinking—the elephant in the room that is not being addressed—is the profound difference between a religion that sacrifices a goat to a spirit god, and Western religion. Why is it, for instance, that the primitive religions that preceded ours (and in some cases survive) are so mired in animism? Why is it that in all the religious tribes that Boyer describes, except ours, there do not seem to be any tribal sceptics, let alone atheists? To equate primitive beliefs with ours is like saying that because you can show a similarity between the intuitive physics of primitive tribes and that of the Western world—*you have thereby explained* why contemporary physics has reached its present dizzying heights.

Anthropological evolutionists like Pascal Boyer assume that they are studying the building blocks of the origin of religion. Yet, obviously, for whatever reasons, these are building blocks that were never developed to anything approaching the level of our contemporary sophistication. How, one wonders, can these anthropologists be sure that the reason that these primitive tribes did not advance to our level was because *they did not possess the necessary building blocks to begin with*; and that if they really want to understand our Judaeo-Christian religion, *they have to look elsewhere*? Or, to put it another way, since these primitive tribes and our Judaeo-Christian civilisation wound up in such indisputably different places, how can anthropologists know that they started out at a roughly comparable level?

In short, brilliant as it is, there is nothing psychodynamic about Boyer's explanation. While he does talk about the unconscious—he calls it the "basement"—it is clearly the cognitive, information-processing, computational unconscious he is referring to. His methodology, as he frankly says, is that of the social scientist, someone trying to explain vast trends in humanity; someone, by definition, who will bypass the individual in the hunt for general truths. Thus, concludes Boyer, there is no one God, no one religion, only a certain evolutionarily shaped, cognitive template predisposing people everywhere to culturally tailored religious behaviour. He can be therefore masterful when he points out the often tragic conflict between the insistence of institutionalised religion on uniform doctrine and the insistence of local culture on particularity. He can offer a wonderful explanation of why it makes a difference whether you adopt your parent's or your culture's religion or a foreign one. To wit: religion is valuable because it offers a storehouse of social, coalitional information pertaining to a broad, relevant network of trustworthy peers, and intuitively it does not make sense to trade that in for an intriguing but untested system of beliefs that can offer no such benefits. To put it another way, it is much easier and time-saving to stay with what you know than to make a late-in-life switch (like struggling to learn and speak a new language when there is no particular advantage in doing so).

In short, I do not think Pascal Boyer realises that there is a similar tension between the social scientist's insistence on statistically precise group explanations and the individual's need for a custom-made life narrative making sense only to him or her. It is here that the experienced clinician, immersed in the disciplined study of the limitless range of human subjectivity, with the full array of a century of psychodynamic insights at his or her disposal, can make a singular contribution.

The search for supernatural consolation

Nicholas Humphrey is a distinguished theoretical psychologist who happens to be an evolutionist, but who takes yet a different perspective on religion than either Pascal Boyer or Daniel Dennett. His book, *Leaps of Faith*, is an extraordinary blend of bold creative thinking, crystal-clear science writing, sprinkled with common sense, compelling analogies (reminiscent of Richard Dawkins), and lightly worn but awesome scholarship. His quiet, authoritative voice cannot help but command respect.

He is not only unabashedly sceptical when it comes to paranormal claims, but he believes, based on logic and experimental evidence, they "cannot be right". His brilliant, if controversial, insight, after devoting years of study to thousands of so-called paranormal phenomena, is simply that they are *overly designed*. Why, he wants to know, must there be these arbitrary (magician-like) conditions for its manifestation? Why must the lights be out for the spirits to come to the medium? Why are so much of the paranormal forces in the universe directed towards card-reading and tea leaves? Why is it that every test ever performed by an optometrist, vision scientist, or experimental psychologist—all those who are professionally engaged in studying the limits of perception—have never reported the occurrence of a miraculous, science-defying event? Why do spirits only manifest themselves to people who already believe, such as clairvoyants, and never (other than already convinced paranormal investigators) to anyone else?

At bottom, Nicholas Humphrey believes (and I tend to agree with him) that people yearn for facts and theories that determine that the universe is the way they want it. They cannot accept that they cannot escape the limits of science and manifest reality and cannot exert control over how the future—especially their death, along with other misfortunes—turns out. In the final analysis, says Humphrey, religious people, by one name or another, are doomed to believe in what he calls *soul power*.

Religion as a natural science

Although he claims to be only a philosopher, Daniel Dennett, in his remarkable new book, *Breaking The Spell*, comes across as a genuine polymath: an expert in religion, evolutionary psychology, cognitive science and the emerging discipline of cultural evolution (created by Richard Dawkins) called mimetics. Like Pascal Boyer, he is careful not to show disdain for any particular religion. An acknowledged atheist, he is less angry and more studiously deferential than Richard Dawkins. But like Richard Dawkins, he is political in his own way, as well as an activist. What he wants is nothing less than to reeducate the world when it comes to religion.

Along with Richard Dawkins (*The God Delusion*) and Christopher Hitchens (*God Is Not Great*), Daniel Dennett is one of the preeminent religious polemicists of the day. An unabashed armchair theoretician, he is not above using his considerable academic cachet to conduct an occasional internet survey on whatever aspect of religious behaviour happens to interest him. A professed lover of the humanities, he appears to be immune to the fundamental religious ideology—what Freud called the oceanic feeling—and what Dennett refers to as the need for supernatural consolation. Although it follows he is less threatening, he is also less inspirational, less open about how he really feels than Richard Dawkins or Christopher Hitchens or, for that matter, Carl Sagan. Undoubtedly heartfelt and passionate—it is more about his ideas than the deep feelings the ideas stand for. Compared to Richard Dawkins, Sam Harris, or the late Carl Sagan—who are like modern-day Darwinian bulldogs (à la Thomas Huxley)—Daniel Dennett is like an exuberantly well-intentioned ACLU advocate for civil discourse.

I include Daniel Dennett because, brilliant as he is, his work personifies the excesses and fallacies of the contemporary, evolutionary psychologist. He equates, for example, evolution's unconscious design—what Richard Dawkins memorably called *the blind watchmaker* (that is, natural selection)—with a non-living, mechanical, unconscious that might as well be inanimate. (We are reminded here that one of the hats Dennett wears is that of prominent computer scientist.) By so doing, Daniel Dennett fails to recognise that the human psychodynamic unconscious is a living, non-mechanical, and autonomous system. He forgets that without the help of a team of human experts there could be no examples of a supposedly intelligent machine—such as a world-class, chess-playing computer that, without the designer's program, the computer can have no chance of ever achieving autonomous self-awareness.

Over and over again, Daniel Dennett struggles to show how what seems in history to have been designed (notably, the most fundamental rituals of folk religion) could really have arisen—by the unconscious spreading of memes—in the same way evolution has always proceeded, with no foresight, by trial and error. In this way, adaptations over vast stretches of geological time could have been incrementally built up.

We see that Daniel Dennett has a revolutionary agenda: to translate consciousness into mechanical, computer-friendly terms; to define all thinking as being cognitive, in either a rational or an irrational way, much as an expert programmer might evaluate a new piece of software. In this manner, millennium-old mysteries of the human mind seemingly dissolve into a series of pragmatic engineering questions. Does it function? Is it doing what it was designed to do—(designed, that is, in the case of evolution, by natural selection)—if not, why not? What needs to be done to fix it? Questions that irresistibly lead to the cutting-edge fields of artificial intelligence and robotics.

It follows the programmatic attempt to reduce the mind to the algorithmic workings of a modern computer (in the spirit of Daniel Dennett and Steven Pinker) will come at the price of a great reduction. If cognition is the key, then the profound difference between animal minds must be somehow relegated to the category of non-minds, or protominds (as with chimpanzees), or pre-human emergent minds. Animal psychologists do this by focusing almost exclusively on the various ways in which the minds of higher animals seem to resemble our own. They create the impression that animals are only thinking if they remind us of ourselves. They do not seriously consider that they may be thinking all the time (as we do), but in a radically non-human way. They are like developmental psychologists—waiting for that magical emergent moment—when the human infant will manifest the first precursor of a budding cognition. They do not consider that, for all we know, infants, analogous to higher mammals, prior to and after those prized transformative moments, may be deeply engaged in a profoundly different, howsoever undeveloped, mode of reacting to, processing, and appraising the world they live in.

From this perspective, we can see that one of the things that made Freud's idea of a dynamic unconscious so compelling was that here for the first time in history a truly new kind of mind was being proposed: one that was disturbingly non-rational, self-contradictory, undifferentiated, and driven by instincts that nevertheless seemed to have a real say in how we think when we are being at our most conscious and most cognitive. By doing away with all such explanatory structures that were deeply counterintuitive, evolutionary psychologists find themselves with the paradox of having to explain how at the heart of quantum mechanics there is something called *quantum strangeness*.

Daniel Dennett is at his best when he is most speculative. (It is here where his brilliance as a philosopher is most evident.) The scope of his ambition is enormous. He wants to redefine the psychology of religion in terms suitable for neuroscience and biology, terms that are potentially "testable". To begin by translating human agency into what he calls the intentional stance—to thereby establish a much-sought-after link with programmed intelligence. At his best, he can be ingenious, as in this touching example involving his five-year-old daughter. She has managed to crush her fingertips and is in great pain. A desperate

Dennett, who is driving her to the hospital, concocts an on-the-spot placebo. He tells her "a secret": if she tries real hard, and thinks real hard, she can push the pain in her crushed fingertips into his hand. And—seemingly like magic—says Dennett, the secret works! But only for a few minutes. So he asks her to do the secret again, and again it works, but for not quite as long. Behind the "secret", surmises Dennett, was a kind of instant hypnosis and behind that was the evolutionary principle of imprinting. This is a critical period of learning when animals are hardwired to imprint, upon the first appropriately sized moving animal they encounter, the inborn image of mother and to react accordingly for the rest of their lives. Generalising from that, Dennett speculates that human beings similarly are hardwired to believe in "superhuman adults": those invisible, magical, rescuing giants who never fail to answer their cries for help. What he is really saying is that evolution has programmed children—as a survival mechanism—to be extraordinarily gullible. Why? Because if they instinctively believe just about any fairytale their parents find necessary to tell them, they will naturally do what they are told during the critical years when they cannot be expected to think for themselves and to fend for themselves; when, in the classic example, children cannot afford to learn by trial and error, it is unhealthy to place their hands on a hot stove. So, knowing this, a distraught Dennett creates an *ad hoc* secret involving magical pain transfer and his equally distraught small daughter, desperate to be rescued once again by the superhuman adult, swallows it on the spot! It is only a short step from that, claims Dennett, towards understanding how it came to be that the overwhelming majority of children grow up to adopt, out of a choice of many thousands, the religion of their parents.

I do not believe Daniel Dennett realises, at this point, that he is showing an idea suspiciously close to a fundamental psychodynamic conception of the infant's psyche. In a very famous paper, *The Transformational Object*, the brilliant psychoanalyst Christopher Bollas ties our susceptibility to mystical and religious oceanic feelings, to the original psychic merger between infant and mother. To a time when every new sensation, every perceivable alteration of their inner world, seemed like a magical transformation coming from without. It is not surprising that insights like this cannot be allowed. Everything that is not evolutionary psychology or neuroscience is relegated to the dismissive category of "folk psychology". In place of psychodynamics, Daniel Dennett leans on evolutionary anthropologists such as Scot Atran and Pascal Boyer. He cites the psychologist Nicholas Humphrey, whom he says has offered the best hypothesis to explain the evolutionary benefits of the placebo effect: that is, since it is wasteful for our immune system to respond to every false alarm, it will tend to hold back; it will wait for a clear signal that legitimate help is near—such as when we are in the presence of a Shaman, a healer, someone in authority *in whom we believe*—at which point our immune system will go all out.

It is thus that Nicholas Humphrey explains the power of the placebo. I admit, when I first read this, I was struck with how ingenious it was (a reaction I often have when I read Nicholas Humphrey). I immediately thought of my own field of psychotherapy and the guiding principle of transference, the irresistible tendency to trust, sometimes far too much, the authority of the therapist. Could that be a placebo effect? I thought of the patients I have treated who were terminally ill, who sometimes, when there was objectively very little hope—when therefore *every one of their resources was desperately needed to stave off the end*—would rally magnificently (psychologically, that is). Could that be the placebo effect?

Building on this, Daniel Dennett speculates that the so-called God centre of the brain—if there is one—might have survived because it provided the "only health insurance available". In other words, if it is true that belief in authority is required in order to really jumpstart our immune system, then suggestibility to Shamanic medicine as the only medicine available may well have had survival value: that is, those who did not have a God centre in their brains died!

To give Daniel Dennett his due, this also is ingenious. But he is by no means done. His remarkable, wide-ranging book is chockfull of novel ideas as to how to link religion to natural science. One of his ideas is that only observable, detectable differences make a difference; and if you cannot tell the difference, there is no difference! It is an idea originally made famous by Allan Turing in his creation of the *Turing Test*: if a tester cannot tell the difference between the answers given by a machine and the answers given by a human being, then the machine must be considered intelligent.

In an imaginative leap, Dennett applies this standard to the question of belief, in particular to the notorious spy case of Kim Philby, a senior officer in the British Intelligence Service. By 1951, he had fallen under suspicion of being a double agent, of secretly operating as a traitor working for the Soviet KGB. Eventually, he was found not guilty due to insufficient evidence, but he was refused reinstatement. Disgruntled, Philby moved to Beirut, upon which new evidence surfaced confirming he had indeed been a double agent. When confronted with this in Beirut by the British Intelligence Service, he fled to Moscow where he allegedly spent the remainder of his life working for the KGB. Whereupon a new theory emerged! Could it be that when Philby arrived in Moscow, claiming to be a disgruntled British spy who now wanted to defect in earnest, he was only *pretending*. Could it be that when Philby originally was exonerated, the British Intelligence had gone to him with a new, amazingly duplicitous assignment—*pretend* to be disgruntled and *pretend* to be defecting to Moscow!

Here Dennett draws a characteristically bold conclusion: it *didn't matter* whether he was truly a British patriot "pretending to be a disgruntled agent, or a truly loyal Soviet agent pretending to be a loyal British agent (pretending to be a disgruntled agent). He would behave in exactly the same ways in either case"!

At this point, I must point out the radical behaviourist philosophy which underpins this admittedly diabolically clever example. Dennett is saying that, in effect, that if you can't see the difference, there is no difference. If you can't tell if Kim Philby is really a loyal British agent pretending to be a disgruntled defector, or if he is really a loyal Soviet agent pretending to be a loyal British agent pretending to be a disgruntled defector—it makes no difference. But how can that be the case? How can it make no difference if someone were really a loyal British agent or only pretending to be one? Isn't that the difference between giving only harmless information or calculated misinformation and giving crucially vital information? Isn't that the difference between being a sociopathic imposter who barely succeeds in fooling someone that he's a doctor—for example, Leonardo DiCaprio in *Catch Me If You Can*—and someone who is a doctor? Isn't there still a meaningful difference even if the impostor somehow happens to know just as much and can perform just as competently as the real doctor? Isn't that difference the difference between someone who is trustworthy and someone who is not? Which is why no patient would ever go to such an impostor therapist knowingly and no government would ever knowingly recruit someone—who was in fact a counter agent—to be a spy.

One of Daniel Dennett's most original ideas is the concept of *belief in belief* (Dennett, 2006, p. 6). Religious people, he points out, do not so much believe in religion as they believe in the value of belief. He notes how often it is hard—not only for outsiders but for the religious believers themselves or even the religious teachers—to know the real difference between what they are professing to believe and what they really believe. This is because, he says, the terms of religion—in order to be made as immune as possible to subsequent sceptical inquiry, reality-testing, and possible scientific refutation—are deliberately crafted to be not only not falsifiable, in Karl Popper's original sense, but also somewhat incomprehensible. To overcome this problem and maintain the continuity of religious doctrine, authorities have over the ages pragmatically insisted (as, for example, in Catholicism) on the rote professing of purported beliefs as being tantamount to being considered faithful.

In other words, it becomes necessary in a strict religious culture to believe what you are told you are supposed to believe and to do what you are supposed to do: that is, to adhere to and to practise the required rituals. This is why, Dennett astutely observes, most believers, along with a surprising number of supposed experts, would have a hard time passing a tough multiple-choice test on what they really believe. The emphasis, concludes Dennett, is *not on understanding but on professing belief and practising belief.*

If you accept Daniel Dennett's premises—that cognition is the foundation of all thinking—then his logic is unassailable. But if you look at what he leaves out—everything about real life that is irrational, emotional, conflicted, sometimes barely conscious yet profoundly meaningful—then he is far less persuasive. It follows Dennett's critique of religion as being really about belief in belief, is weakened once we descend from the realm of abstraction and being in real life consequences. For when we look at everything a person must give up in order to become a priest or minister, it seems clear something substantive and specific at the core of their belief system must be driving them. If, by contrast, we see someone professing belief in a New Age creed, a creed for which no sacrifices are required, it seems equally clear to assume we are dealing with a fancy rather than a commitment.

One of the strengths of the psychodynamic approach is that it takes seriously the question of *meaning*. It does not start with the end point of behaviour. When Dennett says, "When it comes to interpreting religious avowals of others, everybody is an outsider"—he is overlooking the well-known ability of psychotherapy to get inside someone's head. He is failing to realise it is possible to differentiate between words and verbal behaviour and between unconscious subtext and unspoken meaning. He appears never to have had the deep empathic resonance of reverberating to another's unconscious—with the result you have a much better chance of getting inside their head than if you only philosophically analyse and observe their behaviour.

In short, Daniel Dennett does not seem to realise that part of his outsider bafflement is a self-induced projection of his own determinedly detached, cognitive stance. It is ironic that Dennett himself was originally in the forefront when it came to demolishing the then fashionable radical behaviourism associated with the late B. F. Skinner and replacing it with the rising discipline of cognitive science. This was the doctrine that allowed for the first time certain fundamental cognitive constructs, entities, and putative structures in the mind that could not be directly observed—but which could be inferred based on precisely measured, quantifiable observables (fMRI brain scans)—to be recognised. Note that here the cognitive neuroscientist and the radical behaviourist are both equally relying on the baseline of quantifiable behaviourism; but in the newer cognitive science, the investigation is allowed to make the step of going from the observed to the unobserved. (The classic example being Noam Chomsky's seminal idea of an unseen language template or module informing all of the infinitely variable, multicultural language permutations).

Despite this role as a pioneer in the growth of cognitive science, Daniel Dennett, in his 1991 *tour de force*, *Consciousness Explained*, seems to unabashedly return to the most radical of all types of behaviourism—artificial intelligence—or as he sometimes calls it, "mechanical thinking". He does nothing less than aspire to reduce the infinitely rich phenomenology of self-aware consciousness to a series of increasingly sophisticated, hierarchically positioned computer programs. His consciousness explained is really a concentrated effort to *explain away* the subjective phenomenon of consciousness by reducing it to a matter of differentiating between one behavioural reporting mechanism and another.

We see that Daniel Dennett is once again insisting that if you can't differentiate between the behavioural reports of a machine and that of a person, *there is no difference*. And here we are right back to the Turing Test and to artificial intelligence. (Disclosure: the very first paper I wrote on this subject—"A Psychoanalyst Takes the Turing Test"—was published in 1990, and recently anthologised in Franco Salzone's *Neuroscience and Psychoanalysis*.) To adhere, as Dennett obviously does, to such a rigid stance is to be immune to criticism. Thus, when the prominent philosopher of science John Searle published his famous Chinese Room assault on the computer model of the mind—that a man who could perfectly manipulate the symbols to the proper Chinese words, but who could not read or understand Chinese, could not be said to be conscious—Dennett had an almost instant reply: in effect, okay, if you like, I'll add another program to the computer that translates the Chinese words, so that the meaning can be understood.

He doesn't seem to see that he could build an infinite series of such self-reflective programs, and Searle's idea would equally apply. He doesn't realise that to abandon the psychodynamic dimension is to get lost in a maze of ultimately self-defeating professorial logic. And once again, I am reminded of what my old teacher, Paul Edwards, once said, "Some ideas are only believed in the classroom!"

"I do not think God plays dice with the universe"

Albert Einstein, the father of modern cosmology, famously said he did not believe that chaos and indeterminacy could lay at the heart of the cosmos. The general theory of relativity was his glorious answer to the greatest of all questions—"How could something come from nothing?" It is a question with many forms and is often unconsciously framed as—how could something as richly diverse and seemingly infinite as our universe pop up spontaneously from a nothingness? Since Einstein, modern cosmology has attempted to answer that immemorial conundrum by reducing the contrast between something and nothing to as infinitely negligible a difference as theoretically possible. In other words, not how could something as infinitely various as our universe ever emerge from a black hole of absolute nothingness but—how might the faintest imaginable quantum fluctuation somehow give rise to an only slightly more complicated energy arrangement? Framed this way, the difference between the quantum fluctuation in the hypothetical void that preceded the Big Bang—and the resulting initial starting conditions that would now serve as catalyst for the Big Bang—would be almost infinitesimal.

One of the clearest and most compelling accounts of our modern scientific account of the creation myth is *The Void* by the physicist Frank Close. What exactly is the void? It is nothing but the contemporary answer to the age-old question—can a perfect vacuum exist in nature? Or as Frank Close says—"if you take away the Earth, the Moon, the stars—everything material—what remains?" (Close, 2007, p. 3). An award-winning populiser of science in addition to being a distinguished theoretician, he is, for me, the Richard Dawkins of particle physics. Like Dawkins, he has at his command a wonderful arsenal of mental imagery to convey the profundities of quantum strangeness and like Dawkins, as an added bonus, he can be a masterful storyteller.

Frank Close never loses sight of his central narrative thread—where did the universe come from? His book opens and closes with the same baffling, cosmological question. He neither skirts the intractability of the enigma nor offers premature solutions: such as (as it seems to me) Victor Stenger's explanation (creative though it is) that something came from nothing because nothing is "more unstable (hence susceptible to symmetry-breaking) than something" (Stenger, 2009, p. 239). (My admittedly philosophical but non-technical objection to this is—even if true—a quantum fluctuation of nothingness unstable enough to precipitate a something as momentous as the Big Bang *cannot be just nothing*.) Or, as Frank Close, having conducted his survey, says, "Everything may thus be a quantum fluctuation out of nothing". But if this is so, he immediately reflects, "I am still confronted with the enigma of what encoded the quantum possibility in the Void". In other words, if, as modern cosmology tells us, the Void is really filled with seething energy, with quantum fluctuation, howsoever infinitesimal, with the elusive Higgs field—that cannot be nothing. Or, more simply put, just before the Big Bang, what was the world like? Did space and time exist prior to the Big Bang or were they created afterwards?

It is Frank Close's special gift to capture the human element in this greatest of all cosmological dreams. By framing his book as the sustained passionate quest to answer the greatest of all questions—who or what created the cosmos—he manages to construct a narrative as scientifically precise as it is personally meaningful. His book, in short, is alive with a dynamic sense of a cosmos being born, trying to be born, or exponentially growing. He never fails to highlight the undeniable, if utterly impersonal mystery of his cosmological drama. He is magnificent when it comes to translating profoundly complex ideas (for example, symmetry-breaking)—how the world might emerge from, if not nothing, then the simplest beginning (for example, "an amorphous plasma")—into the most lucidly accessible terms imaginable. And, finally, he can be equally masterful when it comes to inviting us into the subatomic world of quantum strangeness.

The anthropic principle

Among the many attempts to forge a scientifically respectable account of our cosmos' creation, perhaps none is so blatantly subjective, so unashamedly anthropomorphic as this principle. For this principle, in its simplest, most general form, points out that the universe we perceive about us must be of such a nature as will produce and accommodate beings who can perceive it. This, of course, is so self-evident as to be almost tautologous. What is not tautologous is the additional claim that—because the initial starting conditions of our Big Bang have been determined to be so extraordinarily precise—they must have been *designed*. Which immediately raises unanswerable, metaphysical questions as to who or what designed the cosmos? A god? An intelligent designer? An extraterrestrial intelligence incomparably more advanced than we are? Or was it the outcome of some kind of a "natural selection" of universe, as suggested by the physicist, Lee Smolin, in his remarkable book, *The Life of the Cosmos*.

John Barrow, one of the original architects of the Anthropic Principle, carries this further. He believes we may never know why the universe was so fine-tuned for our existence because we may never know what preceded the Big Bang. In his recent scintillating book, *The New Theories of Everything*, he exhaustively reviews the latest and most sophisticated attempts to arrive at a final theory of physics. Although duly respectful of these efforts, he does not seem to believe they will succeed. He points to the fact that although our minds seem evolved to deal with basically three dimensions, it is conceivable that there could be an unimaginable number of possible dimensions to possible worlds. There may presumably be other physics with different fundamental laws in other parts of our universe. If space is infinite, as it may well be, there could be an infinite number of conceivable worlds, a number that by definition will forever elude the grasp of our necessarily finite minds.

Although he does not say it, John Barrow comes close here to the philosophic position—as articulated by Colin McGinn—called *Mysterianism* (McGinn, 1999, pp. 68–76). This is the radical view, that because of the natural restraints all biological organisms have, our minds may be *cognitively closed* to certain ways of perceiving and knowing. It may, in short, be an act of incredible hubris to believe we may be capable of actually comprehending the entire universe.

As intriguing as the idea of mysterianism may be, it is vulnerable to its own critique. For how can one ever be sure that one day a final theory, a theory of everything, will not be arrived at? How can one say that because something is counterintuitive, we cannot understand it? Isn't the history of twentieth-century physics filled with the discovery of one profoundly counterintuitive idea after another? From Einstein's special and general theories of relativity to the *Alice in Wonderland* world of quantum strangeness, to the even more unimaginable idea of contemporary string theorists?

Although no one will deny modern science is rife with baffling gaps and anomalies, it is also true that is the way great discoveries have been made. An anomalous result is announced—the Michelson-Morley experiment, for example, challenging the concept of an ether—and an Albert Einstein uses that to dramatically conclude that the ether presumed for years to pervade the universe as the medium through which an instantaneous gravitational attraction is conveyed, does not exist! What previously was seen as anomalous becomes the catalyst for the discovery of a deeper theory. When Einstein in 1905 gave the world its most famous equation, $E = MC^2$, no one, most of all Einstein himself, could conceive that he had unwittingly provided a blueprint for the building of the first atomic bomb. And because of the increasingly abstract nature of contemporary physics, landmark theories continue to be constructed that often must wait decades for their predictions to be verified.

As Steven Weinberg has noted in *Facing Up*, there isn't anything in science of which it can't be said something in the future might overturn it. Since the future by definition can never be known, we can't be completely sure that even the most spectacularly successful, predictive, mundane certainty—such as, the sun will rise tomorrow—will not one day be refuted. How then, it may well be asked, can we ever be sure that we will never be able to fully comprehend the universe because we lack the necessary cognitive equipment? To which the only answer seems to be: if we continue to come up with increasingly comprehensive theories satisfactorily explaining more and more of the observable universe, we may assume we are probably on the right track.

John Barrow notes, "We never see simple laws—the symmetry of laws—directly, we see only their outcomes" (Barrow, 2007, pp. 245–246).

It is only the equations which are clean and simple. The real world is messy. The outcomes are always more complicated than the laws. He adds, "There is no known prescription for generating quantum solutions directly from classical ones". In other words, "we can only generate quantum laws—that is, the quantum solution must come from quantum laws".

In spite of all this, isn't the history of unprecedented success of quantum mechanics proof that something profoundly counterintuitive—for which we surely were not adapted by Darwinian evolution (cosmic or biological)—can nevertheless be brilliantly successful? And even if true—even if there were a cognitive modality, an X, which was needed to understand the Theory of Everything and which we lack—why couldn't one day, just by dumb luck, by quantum randomness, prodded, perhaps, by a truly anomalous result, some genius *stumble upon the key factor*? A genius like Richard Feynman who—no matter how fond he was of quipping, "No one in the world understands quantum mechanics"—would immediately know what he had? In other words, no matter how counterintuitive the universe at its deepest level may prove to be—no matter how incapable of being understandably visualised—it may still be possible to hit upon the correct operational principles, to derive valid equations, and, above all, to be able to make successful predictions.

Regarding his more optimistic colleagues, John Barrow comments: "It is trivial to say, as does Steven Weinberg, that everything can be reduced to a few elementary particles and their rules". But this, I believe, is itself a decidedly reductionistic interpretation of Weinberg's philosophy of science. As he makes clear in his wonderful book of essays, *Facing Up*, he is not denying the importance of the various hierarchies and symmetry-breakings that John Barrow is at pains to express. He is not denying that the whole is greater than the sum of its parts. He recognises, as does Barrow, that nature is not organised according to invariant principles of counting, addition, and multiplication, that it is not merely dispersed in discrete quantitative groups with some objects on the left side of the equation and some on the right; that to understand the fundamental constants of nature is not the same thing as to understand the rules of a game such as chess.

Steven Weinberg realises, as does John Barrow, that to comprehend nature's laws as they ascend the various hierarchies of complexity, involves much more than arriving at a new geometric picture of basically similar objects in somewhat different (but imaginable) geometric patterns. It requires the addition of qualitatively different organisational principles. It involves emergent qualities created by ever more complex, interactive symmetry-breakings, incorporating change, time, new perspectives, novel functions, and a broader range of experience.

It follows that a geometric or arithmetic picture of similar objects being endlessly arranged and rearranged will not apply. Here is a better analogy to capture the layered nature of emergent experience. Imagine having just completed your first extended visit to a number of major European cities and you are trying to convey to a friend back home the range and depth of your impressions. Intuitively, you realise you cannot simply add up the miles you have travelled, the cities you have visited, the time you have spent. You must somehow find a way to sum up the cumulative impact of numerous levels of experience, perspectives, and—so far as you are concerned—unprecedented ways of living in the world.

I doubt if someone as philosophically minded as Steven Weinberg would disagree with that. He would not, therefore, view the creation of a Theory of Everything as an exercise in "trivial reductionism". He would see it, as would Carl Sagan, Richard Dawkins, Richard Feynman, and Albert Einstein, as the attainment of some truly majestic knowledge, a kind of DNA of the cosmos. He would no more see it as a demeaning reduction, than he would think—the fact DNA requires the organising principles of embryonic development to explain any outcome—somehow detracts from the majestic status of the double helix as the foundational Rosetta Stone of all life processes.

At the close of *New Theories of Everything*, John Barrow, waxing poetic, says: "Beauty, simplicity, truth, these are all properties that are prospective. There is no magic formula that can be called upon to generate all the possible varieties of these attributes. They are never fully exhaustible". This, it should be said, is an extraordinary book, one of the best philosophical treatments of cutting-edge cosmological thought I have read. He writes beautifully, with a kind of restrained passion— a perfect tone for the material at hand—that actually comes across as cosmologically cool. He writes about cosmology with the same stunning clarity that Richard Dawkins marshals for evolutionary biology. Like Dawkins, he conveys the impression of having gone to the heart of whatever he discusses and, like Dawkins, his analogies are about as perfect as can be. Perhaps most impressive of all, he does not seem defensive in regard to any particular agenda.

Although it is sometimes difficult to know where cosmology ends and religion begins, in the case of John Barrow I could not tell what his religious persuasions—if he had any—were, or even if he was spiritually inclined (it is obvious he is very aesthetically and humanistically motivated). To me, he comes closest to Carl Sagan, but without the proselytising, evangelical passion. What he does seem clearly invested in is the exploration of the non-computable, non-compressible elements in the universe; what he calls the unknowability of the future. He wants to stake out, cosmologically, the areas of knowledge that are not reducible to the quantising, differential equations of physics or to the discrete bits of computability.

Especially revealing is the last sentence of the book, "For to see everything would leave us seeing nothing at all". I think Richard Dawkins and Carl Sagan might counter that the true wonder and beauty of the universe comes, not from basking in confusion, but from hard-won understanding. To his credit, John Barrow is not simply glorifying mystery or celebrating a God of the Gaps. He is engaged in what he believes is most meaningful in our quest to understand the universe. He is, in the best sense of the term, an existential cosmologist.

We have come full circle. What began as a child's question as to what lay beyond the edge of space has ended in a welter of mind-boggling theories. We see through all these explorations the need to make not only sense of our place in the world but to understand the world as it uniquely relates to us. No single equation, no theory, no dazzling fMRI image of the hidden brain can ever accomplish this for us. It must patiently be done, one person at a time, each in his or her own way. If the world is ever to make sense to us, it will do so in the context of a meaningful lived life.

CHAPTER FIVE

Sound bites from the cosmos

To travel from the world in which we live to the realm of high-tech, cutting-edge neuroscience can seem, as I have said, like entering a parallel universe. This book has been about why attempts to join these two universes—the world of experience and the world of measurement—so regularly fail. A central theme has been that psychologists, overly zealous in their quest to impose an idealised experimental control, have unwittingly created an artificial dichotomy that can distort as much as it reveals. Much of the book has been one long argument showing that what social scientists claim to have discovered in their laboratories and with their fMRI machines simply does not do justice to the ever-changing complexities of real life, especially as revealed to the psychodynamically attuned clinician.

In this final chapter, I offer a few examples that personify this conflict and, not incidentally, inspired me to write a book about it.

Robert Provine is an experimental psychologist who in 2000 devoted an entire book, *Laughter*, to a disarmingly simple proposition: that most of what passes for humour in everyday social situations *is not funny*. To prove his hypothesis, Provine recorded countless chance encounters of people waiting at train stations, standing in lines, gathering at the water cooler in offices, milling about in classrooms, cafeterias, and city streets. After exhaustively tabulating and analysing his results, Provine decided that less than fifteen per cent could possibly be judged as "humorous". Many of the exchanges typically eliciting a chuckle or laugh were of the form, "Well, off I go ...", "I'll see you later ...", "I know I should not do this, but I probably will ...". Provine was forced to conclude: humour, at bottom, is an interaction-bonding mechanism, a "social phenomena", and its evolutionary purpose is to relax people in order to facilitate group dynamics.

Provine's simple idea not only struck an immediate chord, but charmed me. Suddenly, all those claustrophobic elevator rides with people I barely knew but had to chat with, all those tedious exchanges with people trapped as I was in interminable lines that never seemed to move—fell into place. What made these encounters so awkward was an intuitive sense that they would be neither pleasant nor engaging. Provine, I suddenly realised, was *not* describing laughter, as he apparently thought, but nervous laughter. He was not describing social humour, he was describing dysfunctional humour. Far from laying bare the roots of humour, Provine was inadvertently but brilliantly depicting the kind of situations in which genuine humour, social or otherwise, *cannot emerge.*

But if social humour is really that unfunny, the question arose— Why do people laugh? Robert Triver's famous principle of reciprocal altruism—"You scratch my back, and I'll scratch yours" (Shermer, 2011, p. 247)—almost immediately suggested itself, with a slight twist: "You laugh at my dumb jokes and I'll laugh at yours". Nervous laughter, from this point of view, was a discreet, collusive bailout manoeuvre, but a bailout from what? It was a question exhaustively studied years ago by the great social psychologist Erving Goffman, who devoted himself to exposing everything that is at stake when people meet face to face. Especially relevant to Provine's research was his gem-like observation that, underlying everyday hospitality, was an unspoken agreement: in effect, "I'll pretend to be more generous than I am, if you pretend to be less greedy and demanding than you are". Goffman's classic example was the person who—entertaining a friend in his or her home—gregariously offers, "Stay as long as you like" (so long as it is understood the guest is not to stay much beyond the normal proprietary time) (Goffman, 1967, p. 97). If both participants just play their parts, as Goffman notes, hospitality can be a simple way that everyone can come across as "nicer than they really are". It is a point beautifully encapsulated in Holden Caulfield's immortal complaint, "Why do I always say 'glad to meet you' to people I hate?"

So now imagine, from this perspective, two of Provine's subjects randomly bumping into each other at a train station. Instinctively, they realise that (even if they knew how) there is no time or space in which to construct a good joke (and most people, not being professional comedians, understandably do not know how). Rather than tell jokes, therefore, they are trying to kid around, to be likable, to buy some good will in the few minutes they have. On some level, they know they have a very short time in which to create a favourable impression that hopefully will linger after they leave. From this point of view, what Provine has done is to document the separation anxiety that typically manifests itself as obviously nervous or false laughter. From a psychodynamic perspective, however, all these "non-joke" jokes immediately make sense. The person, who essentially is afraid he or she will come across as socially maladroit, in order to gain the reassurance of a good will smile, begins (usually without realising it) to compulsively clown around.

By presenting these lame attempts at clowning as serious joke attempts, Provine is giving short shrift to the importance of the underlying anxiety. He is overlooking how much of humour derives from the recounting of embarrassing moments: that is, the empathic embarrassment stirred up in the retelling has nowhere to go except through the escape-valve of vicarious nervous laughter. When Provine's subjects say, "Well, off I go", they mean something like, "Wish me luck, I'm heading straight into the human comedy of life". By trying to construct a scientifically respectable rating system for social humour—which entails viewing his subjects as objectively and dispassionately as possible—Provine is missing the importance of empathic identification. By zeroing in on how a hypothetically detached, objective observer might respond to such flippant remarks, he loses sight of the crucial context. He forgets we are not sitting in a professional comedy club, where we have paid good money to get in and feel entitled to be entertained with top-drawer humour. Nor are we sitting in a room taking a paper and pencil test, administered by a psychologist who is trying to measure our level of sophistication when it comes to comedy. Nor are we sitting in our living room trying to impress our friends by recounting the wittiest remark we have just heard.

But imagine for a moment you are standing on the platform of a train station and bump into someone most likely you would rather have avoided. Suddenly, you are faced with the horrible void of a couple of minutes to fill. Your acquaintance, pointing to the darkening sky, says, "Looks like it's going to rain again". All you can think of is to respond, "Yeah, and wouldn't you know I forgot my umbrella". Which elicits the comeback, "It never rains but it pours". The best you now can do (if you are lucky) is (with a hopeful smile), "Was it Mark Twain or Will Rogers who said, 'Everybody talks about the weather but nobody does anything about it?'" Which (thank God) earns a brief chuckle.

It is one thing to read statistical reports of banal repartee, it is another to have to suffer through it. If you are trying to escape an untenable situation, it is the nearest exit, not the fanciest, that you will head for. What is more, if you are someone who hates to get caught without an umbrella, and if it does look like a storm may be coming, the situation—in the sense that nature may be playing a bit of a joke on you—*can look a bit funny*. And remember there is a huge difference between kidding around with someone you know, who happens to be in the same boat you are, and trying to be funny about a complete stranger. Seen this way, there could not be a better example than Provine's allegedly non-funny subjects of the old saying, in regard to the unexpected contingencies of everyday life—"You had to be there".

If you remember the famous television programme, perhaps the first reality TV show ever—*Candid Camera*—you will know what I mean. If you can catch ordinary people with their guard completely down, in the most outrageous, totally unexpected, and compromising circumstances imaginable, they automatically become humorous. It is immediately apparent that what is funny in no way derives from the participants' sense of humour, but comes from their doomed attempts to make sense of a situation in which they do not know they have been diabolically set up. It is an example of *unconscious comedy*. They are funny in the same way two people bumping into each other at a train station, lamely trying to kid their way out of a socially untenable situation, are funny.

Although Provine shrewdly captures the social ineptness of his subjects, he unfortunately presents his findings as a measure of their sense of humour. This would be like conducting a survey of how people talk about the weather—and then concluding the subject "showed little interest or understanding of astronomy" (which would, of course, ignore the phenomenal interest garnered by countless science shows, by populisers such as Carl Sagan, or Steven Hawking, by best-selling books such as *Cosmos* or *A Brief History of Time*). It would be like secretly tape recording the way people sang or hummed while taking a shower, and then presenting the findings as evidence of their low level of musical appreciation!

It is illuminating to see the difference between the way an experimental psychologist like Robert Provine approaches laughter and the way a professional comedian does. In *Born Standing Up—A Comic's Life*, Steve Martin has written a surprisingly touching, beautiful and disarmingly serious memoir of his slow climb from total anonymity to world fame. His book, like that of most well-loved celebrities, has the advantage of being a great story even before we read the first page. Because we already know how it ends, because the story in a certain sense has already been written by history, because we can clearly remember the feelings it has stirred up in us when it was actually happening, we can sit back and enjoy it.

When the author of the memoir happens to be a gifted and nuanced writer, as is the case with Steve Martin, we are in for a special treat. Perhaps the first thing we see is that the character known to the world as Steve Martin was not invented whole cloth. Instead, it was painfully cobbled together over many years from the selected fallout of a lived life. From childhood years working as an assistant in a Disneyland magic store, to his apprenticeship as an amateur Master of Ceremonies, his early student days as a major in philosophy, his introduction via the daughter of Dalton Trumbo to the delights of high-octane, dinner table conversation, his lucky stint as a fledgling writer on the *Smothers Brothers* television show, his dog days travelling the night club circuit as an unknown comedian honing his craft, his break-in appearances on the Ed Sullivan and Johnny Carson shows, to his ultimate place in the sun as the hottest stand-up comedian in the world.

From the standpoint of our theme, what comes across with a person as extraordinarily complex as Steve Martin is the impossibility of ever pinning down the essence of his success, the way an experimental psychologist might try to do with a single variable. His story is an outstanding example of that unique blend of contingency and destiny that every life is. Impossible to predict, it is a story that no one, not even the greatest of novelists, could have invented. As Steve Martin himself makes crystal clear, it is a story that, starting out as a very young man, he himself could never have envisioned, that began perhaps only as a distant dream, an emerging idea, a hope, a fantasy of a yet unknown person, yet a fantasy that, seemingly miraculously, came to pass. Even though the reader will know the happy outcome long before the young dreamer, the effect can be stunning. That someone can first dream about and then actively become such a cultural icon can seem almost super-human, as though the person had figured out how to biogenetically engineer a type of human being not previously seen. Furthermore, as one reads, one can run the tape in our heads either backward or forward and respond as one pleases to the favourite stimuli of the remembered person. As an added bonus, *no willing suspension of disbelief is required.* With the echoes of the real character reverberating in our mind, it can seem as though we were watching a beloved movie with which we could not be more familiar.

Much of Steve Martin's memoirs, as in all such memoirs, is devoted to showing us all the ways he resembles ourselves. He is at pains to let us know that up until he graduated high school, as far as he could tell, he had no discernible talent. He traces this low opinion of his abilities to his father's adamant refusal to muster the slightest interest in his son's development. So skilful a writer is he that we are soon convinced Steve Martin really was, at least at first, just one of us. We therefore cannot help but root for him, and when he finally does make it, it seems some-how to be *our* victory, too.

For all of these reasons, the memoirs of a famous person can have the eerie effect of witnessing a human identity being born right before our eyes. Unlike that of other people, who already have identities intact when we meet them, this kind of an identity is formed well *after they are adults.* Rather than being the product of developmental, parental, and contingent factors, it appears to have been created imaginatively and aesthetically. It is seemingly an artistic construct rather than being the outcome of a psychological process. But, of course, as every artist knows, behind every creative endeavour there is a period of protracted incubation. The memoir creates the illusion that the process is fully con-scious and intentional. Since primary unconscious factors by definition cannot be known and therefore included, the final smashing triumph can appear as though, rabbit-like, a fully formed identity has just been pulled out of a hat. What initially was confusing to experience for the memoirist, in hindsight seems self-evident. It is why at the end of the book—to his rhetorical question, "What am I, a performer?"—Steve Martin can say simply, "Who wouldn't want to be a performer?"

The answer, of course, is that very few of us want to devote our lives to becoming professional performers and *only* Steve Martin wanted to become the extraordinarily original type of performer he in fact became.

Examples such as this made me realise how precarious it is to try to find and reduce the so-called universals of a lived life—laughter being one of them—to just one or two rigorously controlled variables. To say that is not to ask for less science, but for a more contextual, fuller, richer, and what I have been calling a psychodynamic approach. It means simply to include the salient characteristics that comprise the subjective, dynamic, and unconscious factors that make for a meaningful life.

There are thousands of examples that illustrate the necessity for this. Robert Provine's book on laughter was one that happened to resonate in my mind. Here is another.

"Did you see the gorilla in the room?"

Imagine this: You're watching a one-minute video of two teams of three players each. One team is wearing white shirts and the other black shirts. They are moving about each other in a small room as they toss two basketballs back and forth among themselves. You have been asked to count the number of passes made by the white team. After thirty-five seconds a gorilla unexpectedly enters the room, walks directly through the moving bodies, thumps his chest, and after about nine seconds, exits. Do you think you would see the gorilla?

Not surprisingly, the majority of those who were queried could not imagine missing something as remarkable as a man in a gorilla suit. Nevertheless, as reported by the psychologists Daniel Simons and Christopher Chabris, who conducted the now celebrated experiment, fifty per cent of the subjects do not see the gorilla. They do not see it, not even when asked if they noticed anything unusual. The effect is called *inattentional blindness*: our inclination when attending closely to one task, to become almost blind to a dynamic event occurring right in front of our eyes. As an example, Daniel Simons points to a study by Richard Haines of pilots who were attempting to land a plane in a simulator with the critical flight information superimposed on the windshield. "Under these conditions", says Simons, "some pilots failed to notice that a plane on the ground was blocking their path" (Chabris & Simons, 2010, pp. 19–20).

Michael Shermer has done Simon and Chabris one better. For the past few years, he has been including the gorilla DVD in his public lectures and then asking for a show of hands of those who did not see the gorilla. By "issuing a gender challenge", he discovered he can decrease the figure even more. He tells the audience before showing the DVD that "one gender is more accurate than the other at counting the ball passes, but I won't tell them which so as not to bias the test". According to Michael Shermer, this makes people concentrate harder than ever, "causing even more to miss the gorilla".

Like just about everyone else, when I first heard of this—at a professional lecture by a famous psychologist—I was duly impressed. Here, it seemed, was a truly astounding result. But after a moment thinking this over, as is my wont, my sceptical instinct kicked in; *inattentional blindness*?—didn't that sound suspiciously like the famous psychodynamic concept of *selective inattention* introduced over sixty years ago by the great American psychiatrist Harry Stack Sullivan in his classic text *The Interpersonal Theory of Psychiatry*? Was this, I wondered, just another example of cognitive psychology's penchant for appropriating a basic idea that had been around for a very long time, renaming it, and then claiming it as its own?

When I therefore tried to rethink the celebrated gorilla experiment from the standpoint of real people and real life, I did not have far to look. If you are a sports fan, as I am, you will recall what happens when any kind of an unusual attention-getting event happens at a crowded arena: within seconds, all eyes turn toward the bonus entertainment. It is a cliché in prime time sports that the fist fight in the stands, the self-proclaimed world's greatest fan who bursts onto the playing field, the streaker at Wimbledon, or even the errant pigeon who manages to somehow disrupt the game, will have no trouble stealing the show. So instead of pondering the mystery of why people didn't see the gorilla, I began to wonder why none of the players on the two teams who were passing the two basketballs back and forth had apparently not noticed the gorilla who had strolled into their midst.

Since it was, of course, inconceivable that could possibly have happened in real life, it was obvious its omission was an important part of the experiment. I immediately realised that here was another case where unknowing participants were being duped by the experimenter. Not only did all six basketball players have to have been stooges in the experiment, but by deliberately pretending not to see the gorilla in their midst, they were delivering the subliminal social cues that nothing untoward is happening, that the only event worth looking at was what they were looking at—that is, six basketball players simply throwing two basketballs around. But nothing could be further from the truth! The experimenters were doing everything in their power to set up the participants so *that they do not see the gorilla*. Once you begin to view this experiment as an example of covert social manipulation, which I believe it is, things no longer look the same.

If you doubt this, just try to recall what happens should you walk into a room, or any public place and you notice everyone seems to be doing the same thing—looking down at the floor, or up at the ceiling or simply pointing to something that just happened. Being social animals, we immediately want to investigate, at least initially, what it is that is keeping everyone in synch. This means—in terms of what is worth noticing and what is not—that we cannot help but be influenced by what everyone around us is doing. And that means, regarding our experiment, that perhaps the single most important event occurring in the one minute video, although it is of course deliberately downplayed, is that all of the six basketball players act for all the world as though *the man in the gorilla suit who entered their midst, thumped his chest and exited after nine seconds did not exist.*

Again, if you doubt this, imagine an actual New York Knickerbockers basketball game being played at Madison Square Garden, in the midst of which a man in a gorilla suit strolls onto the court. Would there be a single fan in the packed arena who either did not immediately see it or soon hear about it from an excited neighbour?

To look at the gorilla DVD this way, from the standpoint of covert manipulation, is for things to fall into place. It makes sense for a viewer, instructed to pay close attention to the hand-eye coordination required to catch a basketball moving quickly through the air, coming from a variety of angles, to exclude everything from his or her vision except the patch of flesh and muscle stretching from a player's pelvis to his diaphragm. It makes sense, therefore, for the viewer to shrink his or her normal panoramic field of vision down to a narrow band where only hands, balls, and the colour white matter. And note that although the intruding gorilla thumps its chest, it presumably *does not catch a single ball*. Only a moment's thought will tell us why. Were the furry forearms, massive hands to enter your selected field of vision, it is hard to imagine that it could possibly escape notice. But it is comparatively quite easy to imagine that the distinguishing features of the gorilla—the head, shoulders, and chest—all being safely out of range of the targeted visual area, will escape notice.

To illustrate the point, imagine this: You are watching a one-minute video—not of two teams of three players each, but of a private club room whose members are both entering and leaving. Some of the members are wearing white shoes and the others are wearing black shoes. You are instructed to count the number of white shoes that either enter or exit the room. After thirty-five seconds a trained eagle is released that buzzes the heads of all the members for about eight seconds and then flies out of the room. Would it surprise you very much if not that many viewers noticed the eagle? And if not, isn't the gorilla DVD in reality just a minor variation in principle of that very same experiment?

Or consider this: a midget, about three feet tall, not a gorilla, enters the room after thirty seconds and starts catching the ball. Do you think as many viewers would now fail to see the three-foot midget—*who had entered the targeted field of vision*—as failed to see the gorilla? Or think about this: instead of two teams of three players each moving about each other—the point of which, I believe, is to *blur the effect of the gorilla's body entering their midst*—having each team remain stationary as they toss the two basketballs back and forth. Do you think the gorilla entering their midst would as easily go unnoticed?

Finally, it is worth noting some of the questions that are *not* asked. What about the fifty per cent of viewers who *did see* the gorilla? Did they possess some special perceptual acuity that allowed them to spot the hirsute intruder? And if so, what was it? Or was it simply, as I suspect, that the amount of intense concentration required to count the number of passes made by the white team was such that, after a while, it became increasingly easy for one's attention to deviate from the restricted visual range? And once it did, it immediately became impossible not to notice the gorilla.

We are back to where we started from, to Stanley Milgram and his famous electro-shock experiments—where the question becomes: To what extent does the experimenter (often unknowingly) create the very results he or she is claiming to have objectively discovered?

It's alive

At Astor Place subway or Union Square train station on occasion you will see a strange creature. Over six feet tall, fully formed, sculpted like a man, it stands frozen in posture, one arm extended, the other pulled back. The skin on its face and hands appear to be covered with a gold paint. It is of course too unusual to pass by, but not the kind of thing you'd want to approach either. Instinctively you realise it's alive. The man is a street performer who is impersonating a man who has mysteriously become petrified, or who has metamorphosed into a statue. If you are like me you marvel at not only the skill but the extraordinary discipline it must take to remain that motionless and you wonder what motivates someone to do this?

Almost as unusual and far more entertaining—in the heart of the Times Square subway station—is the beautiful dance between the man and doll. The man, a famous New York local character who has appeared on television in his satin pants and flashy black hat, looks like a gypsy and moves in flawless syncopation with his partner. Seemingly about four and a half feet in height when stood up, with curly blond hair and a Shirley Temple face, she begins lying flat on her back, like a discarded dummy, her feet somehow joined to the man's shoes. Suddenly, a cheerful mazurka blares from the huge boom box to the fascination of the inevitable crowd that gathers to watch, and the man springs into action. Instantly, with a flick of his wrist, the doll, as though summoned to life, leaps forward. Amazingly, she seems as accomplished a dancer as he is. What he can do, she can do. She can twirl, tango, do backward dips, as she holds tightly to the man's hands. It is obvious there is a bond, a relationship of some kind between the man and the doll, and after a while you may find yourself wondering what else they can do together besides dancing?

What impressed me about these street performers was their uncanny ability—simply by acting out, and apparently taking serious, unprecedented, even surreal relationships to things typically taken for granted—to manipulate the way we see the most familiar of objects. It was performance artists such as these who first made me realise how much more fluid and changeable was our relationship to our world than that which is portrayed by the experimental psychologist. And it was through working with patients who happened to be performance artists that I would be introduced to the inner dynamics of their alternative sensory world. For me, and in terms of our theme, there is no better example of the power of creative subjectivity to recontextualise the way we experience our physical world.

Consider, for example, a very famous performance by Joseph Beuys: *How to Explain Pictures to a Dead Hare*. In Roselee Goldber's haunting book, *Performance: Live Art Since 1960*, there is a picture of him you are not likely to forget. Joseph Beuys, looking supernaturally sad, his face smeared with a gold patina, pieces of earth, dried leaves, is contemplating the corpse of a dead hare that he is cradling in his arms. In the original performance, he is glimpsed behind a storefront window, earnestly trying to get through to the dead rabbit. At one end of the room is a picture, meant to represent perhaps a certain ineffable essence of contemporary art. Now and then he may carry the rabbit up to the painting and rub its paws on the canvas. Or he may simply walk with the rabbit the way one does with a non-responsive, inconsolable baby as he continues to whisper encouragement. I am told that Joseph Beuys can perform this piece, reiterating a brief repertoire of these same dumb actions up to fifteen hours at a stretch. It is part of the art not to tell his bewildered audience what he is doing. It is for us to interpret why he apparently feels it is more worthwhile to explain modern art to a dead hare than to us.

To encounter this kind of art for the first time is like being taken on a sensory roller coaster. And like a roller coaster ride, you have little say in what or how you're going to experience it. You will either like it or not, but you cannot be neutral. Analogously, art such as this will settle for nothing less than a polarising response. It may help to remember that performance art is a child of the volatile, countercultural Sixties. It is determined to do away with traditional narrative structures of every kind, no matter what the cost. Its revolutionary intent is to be as unmediated, unprocessed, and unreflective a medium as possible.

Accordingly, the prospective audience member, who has been invited to be immersed in the experience, is not allowed to choose how far he or she may want to enter. The performance artist, like Joseph Beuys, in order to achieve the immediacy of jazz, is more than willing to sabotage the autonomy of its audience. It is not above cheap sensationalism and shock tactics. It adheres to the revolutionary credo that the means justifies the end. Like Dadaism before it, it seems to revel in depriving the viewer of the crutch of any recognisable frame of reference. To have any chance of appreciating the performance, you must consent to becoming a prisoner of a psychedelic experience. Seen this way, performance art is a happening rather than a work of art, ready to lend itself to sado-masochistic, exhibitionistic acting out if that is what is required.

To achieve its revolutionary aims, the performance artist will even challenge the basic evolutionary integrity of our body, the very foundational frame of how we process the spatial and temporal world around us. While we may not care (at least personally) if Duchamp chooses to elevate a commonplace urinal to the status of a found art object, we can be positively territorial towards the person who wishes to challenge our perception of our own bodies. Like the rebellious child of the Sixties, the performance artist refuses to be ignored.

Being a storyteller by heart, a lover of all kinds of narrative, I was drawn to whatever I found relevant and meaningful from a human point of view. So when I was introduced to performance art, I initially searched for what I could identify as a recognisable narrative arc. I liked Eric Bogosian's *Talk Radio* (which I learned was first considered as a performance art piece), and I especially appreciate the sardonic humour of the subversively original Andy Kaufman. What immediately drew me to the other-worldly tableau of Joseph Beuys trying to explain pictures to a dead hare, was the palpable sense of tragic longing. I didn't need to know the source of his bottomless suffering. I could identify with his loss as easily as I could in the case of my patients. And I could identify with the startling image of Yoko Ono, clothed in a suit made entirely of paper, as she invited first one person and then another of the assembled audience to come up on the stage, take the scissors she provided and cut out and take away as much of her paper suit as they saw fit. I could marvel at the tantalising image of a blindfolded performance artist who nimbly, like a human bat, was trying to catch the balls that were being thrown at him. Or the woman whose naked body was wielded (by the artist who controlled her) as a kind of erotic paint brush on a large, blank sheet of paper. I intuitively realised there was no right and wrong interpretation, and I could effortlessly think up evocative narratives which I would project into what I was seeing.

If I knew what I liked, I was even more certain of what I didn't like. I didn't like, for example—not because it left me cold but because it affected me too much—performers who would use their own bodies as objects of sado-masochistic experimentation and exploration. Too often, I felt, performance artists, utterly lacking in irony, would strike a pose of grandiose self-importance. Performance art, I would realise, relies upon hypnotic repetition to anchor its fleeting sense of reality— perhaps as a reaction formation to its often surreal breaking of traditional boundaries—in the same way religion depends upon rituals. The danger for this kind of a radical art form is that such repetition quickly becomes boring once the necessary realism of the underlying surreal premise is established.

I do not doubt, for example, that the golden man, frozen in space in a corner of Times Square, is a contemporary symbol of a half human/half statue, half alive, half dead, petrified being. But a point comes quickly when it no longer makes sense to continue to experience the spectacle. Besides, what is really mesmerising is not the repetition but the truly extraordinary amount of *suffering, effort, and pain* that the performance artist is willing to endure in order to perform the piece. We watch the man who turns himself into a statue, who hangs upside-down from a precipitous height or submerges himself, wrapped in chains under-water, with a morbid fascination not dissimilar to watching a person threatening in earnest to jump from a building ledge.

In such cases, identification is with the abnormally exciting experi-ence the performance artist is undergoing, but it is not necessarily with the symbolic art of the act. Instead, it is performance art as visual shock theatre, the equivalent of the cinematic action blockbuster. Here, the identification is with the charismatic group leader—the performance artist—and the thrilling prospect of being swept up in primitive group processes (the dynamics of which I explained in detail in *The Portrait of the Artist as a Young Patient*). This promise of titillating sensory libera-tion helps to mask the actual infantile level at which the typical audi-ence member in reality participates: essentially clapping their hands, volunteering to come up on the stage when invited, or engaging in whatever craziness the performance artist requires, such as throwing balls at a blindfolded man. It creates the illusion that as audience we are part of a powerful group process, at the centre of which is a magical leader ushering us into a totally unexpected, surreally novel, but some-how convincing experience.

We immediately see why repetition is a hallmark of performance art: it helps to sustain the illusion that a supernatural force is binding the audience together under its spell. In other words, something inexplica-bly paranormal must be happening—why else would someone hang upside down from a tall building for eighteen hours? Note the charac-teristic lack of development of the central image—Yoko Ono, for exam-ple, sitting on a stage in a paper suit inviting members of the audience to scissor it off her. The performance artist promises a narrative struc-ture, but cannot deliver. He or she is too busy smashing existing sub-texts to supply new ones. Imagine a movie that begins with an image of Joseph Beuys trying to explain pictures to a dead hare—a tableau that seems to resonate with almost infinite possibilities—and then simply goes nowhere. From that perspective, performance art is like a single symbolic act of deconstruction of a traditional narrative frame with this exception: once enacted it immediately repeats, freezes and reifies itself—Joseph Beuys mouthing explanations to a dead hare for up to fifteen hours—as though in sanctification of some genuinely mythic moment or portentous happening that never seems to arrive.

This aura that anything goes creates an illusion of freedom. It can seem as though we are entering a twilight zone of reality, in which there is a new physics, a new grammar of experience unlike anything we have previously encountered. As audience all we know beforehand is that we do not know what to expect next. To such an audience, the performance artist can seem a daring pioneer of a shockingly new way of perceiving the social and political world around us. He may seem like a contemporary Salvador Dali, a sensory contortionist in an unfolding parallel universe of experience. But it is only the genius—like Samuel Beckett (in *Molloy, Malone Dies* and *The Unnamable*), or George Orwell (in *1984*)—who can piece together a convincing alternative world. It is, by contrast, this deconstruction of a known world plus the simultaneous creation of a believable, experiential, and parallel world that is stunning and that is so utterly lacking in the modern day performance artist.

Performance art, in short, is anarchic, not constructive. It builds nothing. Fueled by rage, it manifests no discernible tenderness or love. It implies a narrative, but provides none. The context, if there is one, is simply that of an action symbol. It assumes, and demands, an almost instant iconic status, but it does nothing to earn it. As a narrative form, it is chaotic rather than historical. Nothing of any consequence seems to happen. But there is an inner time: the sense of time passing with a maddening slowness whenever we are undergoing a particularly excruciating experience. So we cannot help but wonder how long can that woman bear sitting on top of that flagpole? How does one possibly endure being submerged, wrapped in chains in icy water (*à la* Houdini)—or hung upside-down from the top of a building?

By seeing to what degree they can torture our sensory, perceptual assumptions, the performance artist pushes the envelope. From a psychodynamic perspective, it may be that the performance artist is reenacting, in the form of a repetition compulsion, an early traumatic experience. It may be that they are trying to sublimate a deadening internalised rage or an artistic addiction to sensory shock and awe tactics.

What does seem clear is that, within the boundaries of performance art, anything goes. Within the boundaries of performance art, there are no boundaries. Nothing is sacred. Performance art may be the most aggressive of all art forms. It can literally assault our perceptions. Its lack of respect for the audience's boundaries can at times seem contemptuous. It is fed by the revolutionary's sense of entitlement. It is perhaps best understood in the context of the sundry social and political revolutions of the Sixties. It is a self-proclaimed anarchic attempt to destroy outdated stereotypes and perceptions. Often with a subtext of brazen manipulation and under the illusion of smashing old subtexts, it inadvertently adds new ones. Without knowing it, the performance artist, within the confines of a supposedly aesthetic framework, becomes a reincarnation of the latent tyranny of the successful revolutionary. Although every artist, at some point, craves the approval of an imagined audience, it is the performance artist who seizes it.

Performance artists, in short, driven to act out their early emotional traumas, attempt to reconstitute their sensory world in a radically new way. Too often, however, they find that the first casualty of their programmatic deconstruction is themselves. With no boundaries to guide them, they wind up in a no-man's land somewhere between highly theatrical, surreal stage effects and old-fashioned, Sixties-style revolutionary acts of anarchy in the name of a new art form (for example, Abbie Hoffman creating a feeding frenzy at the New York Stock Exchange when he suddenly started throwing hundred-dollar bills on the floor). Yet like most revolutionaries, when it comes time to build a new order, they find themselves at a loss. As mentioned, what made modernists like Kafka and Beckett great was this ability to construct a richly detailed, believable, if fantastical, alternative world.

By contrast, the performance artist's descriptive details and narrative actions do little to enhance the performance. Instead of going deeper, they would rather mix mediums, attempting to create a new hybrid. Overly sensitive to the charge that much of what they do is just a sensory circus sideshow of freaks, they justify the chaos they thereby introduce by assuming a spurious gravitas.

From a psychodynamic standpoint, what is noteworthy is that performance art as a whole seems curiously devoid of the gentler side of human nature: there is an absence of love, tenderness, and kindness. Performance art is an angry art, all about freedom from oppression and taboos. It reeks of a fanatical attempt to manipulate and rearrange the sensory, perceptual, social, and political worlds the artists live in. At times maniacally self-indulgent, instead of being about the world, it can be much more about the revenge fantasies of a particular perform-ance artist. While it may traffic in surreal happenings, it is not thereby constraint-free: like every other psychic phenomena, it is the product of a complex organic structure and a dynamic unconscious.

That being said, performance art at its best, as in the case of Joseph Beuys explaining pictures to a dead hare, can be both powerful and unforgettable. But it is disturbing rather than moving. It utterly lacks the capacity to uplift (in the sense of Beethoven), induce exquisite sad-ness (as in Chopin), or inspire (in the manner of a Dostoyevsky). It is a form of protest art presented in the guise of an action performance. Its almost pathological repetitiveness is meant to convince the viewer that whatever the performance artist is doing—because it is so viscer-ally stressful if not unendurable—must be at least *meaningful to him or her*. Which is important in order to dispel the lurking suspicion that the performance artist is at bottom a fool or a lunatic.

It follows that performance art, though disturbing, can be quite lim-ited. My interest here is by no means intended as a commentary on art history. I offer it as a striking illustration of the remarkable plasticity of human subjectivity: how it can bend to its desires or transform even the most fixed constants of our physical environment—our perception of our bodies and its relationship to others. From our psychodynamic perspective, nothing is more important than to always take into con-sideration the subjective element when investigating human nature. It is a central theme of this book that, regrettably, the more scientific the investigation becomes, the less it is interested in subjectivity.

Consider, for example, the cognitivist. Steven Pinker, in his best-selling book *How the Mind Works*, suggests that the computational the-ory of mind is the solution to the age-old mind–body problem. The key analogy he presents is that of software to hardware. He suggests we think of the mind as symbolic information and the brain as incarnated information. From that standpoint, then, the mind (which is what the brain does, according to Pinker) and the brain are simply two different patterns of information.

Looked at psychodynamically, this is at best a questionable metaphor. While it is perfectly understandable how a computer's software and hardware fit together, no one understands how the so-called hardware of the brain is transformed into the software of the mind. To say that both are analogous equations or ratios of information is to simply fall back on semantics. It is hardly enough to say that information processing is going on in both the brain and the mind. A more pertinent question is how does information which is binary and digital (in the sense of DNA sequences) mysteriously become information in the mind—that is not just more quantitatively precise—but is incomparably more multifaceted, meaningful, and complicated.

If we think of the computer software/hardware analogy in terms of physics, the fallacy becomes even more apparent. A computer's software and hardware, while obviously made of different materials, both obey and are completely explainable by the same laws of physics. It is a different story when it comes to the brain and the mind. Consider the subjective qualia that comprise abstract thought. It has no measurable weight, mass, gravity. It is not susceptible to the four fundamental forces of the universe in any known way. While thought does not violate the basic laws of physics, it is also true that the laws of physics do not explain the dynamics of thought. No less a thinker than the renowned mathematical physicist Roger Penrose has said that there is nothing in the laws of physics that remotely suggest how matter could ever become conscious of itself.

Here is a thought experiment. Imagine a computer that, thanks to the extraordinary advances of neuroscientists, was beginning to achieve the long-sought-after dream of becoming conscious of itself. Now put yourself in the emergent mind of such a computer and try to imagine what such an ambient consciousness would be like. Would it perhaps begin to be aware, to have perceptions, of its own printouts? Would it learn to recognise and to identify with the user in front of it? Would it have sensory awareness of its mouse, its menus? Would it begin to contemplate its storehouse of information? And, most crucially in terms of our theme, would such an emergent consciousness in any serious way remind you of your own?

A far more balanced and profound consideration of the computational theory of the mind–body relation, in my view, can be found in Ekbia's *Artificial Dreams*. Torn between being an experienced teacher of computer science and a probing critic of the field of artificial intelligence, Ekbia is searching for a diagnostic sign of originality that can at least differentiate between human and machine intelligence. He wonders if it could be unpredictability, and he proceeds to quote one of his heroes,

Douglas Hofstaeder: "When you throw a paper airplane or dart, it goes exactly where you threw it, except you don't know where it goes until after it lands (too many unpredictable aerodynamic parameters)".

Although this is ingenious, I would like to suggest that unpredictability in itself is not equivalent to originality, if only because of Hisenberg's principle of uncertainty. Every electron, before it enters a new quantum state, has unpredictability as a feature—does that mean an electron is original? The difference, it seems to me, is that human intelligence can *originate* unpredictability—it therefore has what might be called *autonomous predictability*—while the so-called unpredictability of a machine is entirely passive reactive: it is only unpredictable according to the unpredictable parameters its programmers have set for it.

A much more promising difference between human and machine intelligence is when Ekbia refers to "social life forms". Ekbia doesn't really develop this idea, so I will try to do it for him. The intelligence of a social life form obviously involves something more than to be able to carry out an algorithm for an interactive function—which is often considered to be the essence of mechanical thinking—and which is also what a fancy adding machine can do. By contrast, the intelligence of a social life form—how to write and to understand a love letter, an autobiographical essay, a critique of postmodern philosophy, a strategy for solving the problem of homelessness—involves intimate and extensive knowledge of the history of that particular social life form. That kind of knowledge can only come from being *embedded* in an experiential way with the given social way of being and processing.

In short, to return to the example of the world's greatest chess machine, *Deep Blue* defeating the champion Gary Kasparov: when a human being tries to solve a chess problem, there is more to it than just carrying out a series of complicated algorithms correctly. There is also at play the social life form called playing chess. That is to say, there is the sense of an I–You relationship. Of spatial configurations and how they will transform in an imminent future. There is the anxiety of making a mistake on the chess board. The anticipation of your opponent's reaction (whether that opponent is a human being or an IBM chess-playing machine). There is also—following William James's famous metaphor of a penumbra of consciousness—all sorts of half-formed thoughts and vague impressions hovering in the background. There is the sense of the dynamic passage of time. Of having a body. Of having visual perceptions. Of being capable of face recognition. Of having to concentrate. To exercise selective attention. Not to speak of the murky strivings of a dynamic unconscious.

To my mind, the two greatest metaphors for the process of human consciousness—far more resonant than the computer model proposed by Steven Pinker and so many others—was William James's idea of a stream of consciousness, and Sigmund Freud's concept of derivatives of a dynamic unconscious disturbing the free-associative flow of conscious thought.

But let me return to the beginning so as not to be misunderstood. I still love experimental psychology, and enthusiastically attend lectures by cutting-edge neuroscientists. The point of the book is simply that if we really do want to understand how the human mind works, we need more than the language of the computer, of the fMRI machine, and of the laboratory. We need the language of subjectivity—the psychodynamic understanding that can only emerge within the context of a lived life.

REFERENCES

Alper, G. (1990). A psychoanalyst takes the Turing test. *The Psychoanalytic Review, 77*(1): 59–68.

Alper, G. (1992a). Quantum mechanics as subjectivity and projective stimulus. *The Journal of Contemporary Psychotherapy, 19*(4): 315–324.

Alper, G. (1992b). *Portrait of the Artist as a Young Patient.* New York: Insight/Plenum Books.

Alper, G. (2005). *The Paranoia of Everyday Life.* Amherst, NY: Prometheus Books.

Ariely, D. (2008). *Predictably Irrational.* New York: Harper.

Barkow, I., Cosmides, L. & Tooby, J. (1992). *The Adapted Mind.* New York: Oxford University Press.

Barrow, J. D. (2007). *New Theories of Everything.* New York: Oxford University Press.

Beckett, S. (1965). *Three Novels: Molloy, Malone Dies, The Unnamable.* New York: Grove Press.

Bollas, C. (1987). The transformational object. In: *The Shadow of the Object.* New York: Columbia University Press.

Boyer, P. (2001). *Religion Explained.* New York: Basic Books.

Chabris, C. & Simons, D. (2010). *The Invisible Gorilla.* New York: Crown.

Close, F. (2007). *The Void.* New York: Oxford University Press.

Darwin, C. (1859). *The Origin of Species*. [Republished, New York: The New American Library of World Literature, 1958.]

Dawkins, R. (2003). *The Blind Watchmaker*. New York: W. W. Norton.

Dawkins, R. (2006). *The God Delusion*. New York: Houghton Mifflin.

Dennett, D. (1991). *Consciousness Explained*. New York: Black Bay Books, Little, Brown.

Dennett, D. (2006). *Breaking the Spell*. New York: Penguin.

Dostoyevsky, F. (1991). *Crime and Punishment*. (Translated by David McDuff.) New York: Penguin.

Ehrman, B. (2008). *God's Problem: How the Bible Fails to Answer Our Most Important Question—Why We Suffer*. New York: Harper One.

Ekbia, H. R. (2008). *Artificial Dreams: The Quest for Non-Biologic Intelligence*. New York: Cambridge University Press.

Feynman, R. (1985). *QED: The Strange Theory of Light and Matter*. New Jersey: Princeton University Press.

Freud, S. (1901b). *The Psychopathology of Everyday Life*. Standard Edition, VI. London: Hogarth.

Gladwell, M. (2006). *The Tipping Point*. New York: Little, Brown.

Gilbert, D. (2005). *Stumbling on Happiness*. New York: Knopf.

Goffman, E. (1967). *Interaction Ritual*. New York: Pantheon.

Goldbers, R. (1998). *Performance: Live Art since 1960*. New York: Harry N. Abrams.

Guth, A. (1997). *The Inflationary Universe*. Cambridge, MA: Perseus Books.

Haidt, J. (2006). *The Happiness Hypothesis*. Cambridge, MA: Perseus Books.

Haidt, J. (2011). *The Righteous Mind*. New York: Pantheon.

Harris, S. (2004). *The End of Faith*. New York: W. W. Norton.

Hauser, M. (2006). *Moral Minds: The Nature of Right and Wrong*. New York: Harper Perennial.

Hawking, S. (1988). *A Brief History of Time*. New York: Bantam Books.

Hitchens, C. (2007). *God Is Not Great: How Religion Poisons Everything*. New York: Twelve, Hachette Book Group.

Holt, J. (2007). Good instinct: why is anyone an altruist? *New York Times Magazine*.

Humphrey, N. (1996). *Leap of Faith: Science, Miracles, and the Search for Supernatural Consolation*. New York: Basic Books.

James, W. (1981). *The Principles of Psychology*. Cambridge, MA: Harvard University Press.

Kübler-Ross, E. (1969). *On Death and Dying*. New York: Scribner.

Kushner, H. (2004). *When Bad Things Happen To Good People*. New York: Random House.

Laing, R. D. (1970). *The Divided Self*. Baltimore: Penguin.

Libet, B. (1985). Unconscious cerebral initiative and the role of conscious will in voluntary action. *Behavior and Brain Science, 8*: 529–566.

Lorenz, K. (1981). *The Foundations of Ethology.* New York: Simon and Schuster.

Mailer, N. (1997). *The Gospel According to the Son.* New York: Random House.

Mailer, N. (2007). *On God: An Uncommon Conversation,* with Michael Lennon. New York: Random House.

Mailer, N. (2010). *A Ticket to the Circus.* New York: Random House.

Martin, S. (2007). *Born Standing Up: A Comic's Life.* New York: Scribner.

McGinn, C. (1999). *The Mysterious Flame.* New York: Basic Books.

Menand, L. (2002). *American Studies.* New York: Farrar, Straus, and Giroux.

Milgram, S. (1969). *Obedience to Authority: An Experimental View.* New York: Harper.

Nagel, T. (1979). What is it like to be a bat? *Mortal Questions.* Cambridge: Cambridge University Press.

Orwell, G. (1950). *Nineteen Eighty-Four.* New York: Penguin.

Panksepp, J. (1998). *Affective Neuroscience: The Foundation of Human and Animal Emotions.* New York: Oxford University Press.

PDM Task Force (2006). *Psychodynamic Diagnostic Manual.* Silver Spring, MD: Alliance of Psychoanalytic Organizations.

Penrose, R. (2005). *The Road to Reality: A Complete Guide to the Laws of the Universe.* New York: Knopf.

Pinker, S. (1979). *How the Mind Works.* New York: W. W. Norton.

Provine, R. (2000). *Laughter: A Scientific Investigation.* New York: Viking.

Sacks, O. (1973). *Awakenings.* New York: Harper Collins.

Sacks, O. (1995). *An Anthropologist on Mars: Seven Paradoxical Tales.* New York: Knopf.

Sacks, O. (1997). *The Island of the Colorblind.* New York: Knopf.

Sacks, O. (2001). *Uncle Tungsten: Memories of a Chemical Boyhood.* New York: MacMillan.

Sacks, O. (2007). *Musicophilia: Tales of Music and the Brain.* New York: Knopf.

Sagan, C. (1977). *The Varieties of Scientific Experience.* New York: Penguin.

Scalzone, F. & Zontini, G. (2004). *Psychoanalysis and Neuroscience.* Napoli: Liguori Editore.

Shermer, M. (2008). *The Mind of the Market.* New York: Time Books, Henry Holt.

Shermer, M. (2011). *The Believing Brain.* New York: Henry Holt.

Steinhardt, P. & Turok, N. (2007). *Endless Universe.* New York: Doubleday.

Stenger, V. (2009). *Quantum Gods.* Amherst, NY: Prometheus Books.

Sullivan, H. S. (1953). *The Interpersonal Theory of Psychiatry*. New York: W. W. Norton.

Weinberg, S. (2001). *Facing Up*. Cambridge, MA: Harvard University Press.

Zimbardo, P. (2007). *The Lucifer Effect: Understanding How Good People Turn Evil*. New York: Random House.

INDEX

117

For Product Safety Concerns and Information please contact our EU representative GPSR@taylorandfrancis.com Taylor & Francis Verlag GmbH, Kaufingerstraße 24, 80331 München, Germany

Batch number: 08153785

Printed by Printforce, the Netherlands